The Sophia of Jesus Christ
and
Eugnostos the Blessed

The Divine Feminine and The Gnostic Way

by Joseph Lumpkin

The Sophia of Jesus and Eugnostos the Blessed

Joseph Lumpkin

The Sophia of Jesus Christ and
Eugnostos the Blessed:
The Divine Feminine and The Gnostic Way

Copyright © 2014 by Joseph Lumpkin
All rights reserved.

Printed in the United States of America. No part of this book may be used or reproduced in any manner whatsoever without written permission except in the case of brief quotations embodied in critical articles and reviews.

Fifth Estate Publishing, Blountsville, AL 35031

Cover Designed by An Quigley

Printed on acid-free paper

Library of Congress Control No: 2014944930

ISBN: 9781936533459

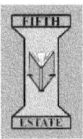

Fifth Estate, 2014

The Sophia of Jesus and Eugnostos the Blessed

Table of Contents

Introduction	7
A Brief Introduction to Gnosticism	12
Defining the Divine Feminine	61
Understanding the Divine Feminine	74
Introduction to The Sophia of Jesus Christ	123
The Sophia of Jesus Christ	135
Introduction to Eugnostos the Blessed	154
Eugnostos the Blessed	159

The Sophia of Jesus and Eugnostos the Blessed

Joseph Lumpkin

Introduction

The treatise of *Eugnostos the Blessed* (50-150 A.D.) and the gospel called, *The Sophia of Jesus Christ*, (50-200 A.D.) are presented together in a single volume, due to their close and undeniable connection. In fact, one borrowed heavily from the other. *The Sophia of Jesus Christ*, also called The **Wisdom of Jesus Christ**, seems to be a later and Christianized version of *Eugnostos the Blessed*, a non-Christian Gnostic text. Separate audiences were being targeted with the two related texts and thus they use different modes of presentation, however the words and ideas remain the same.

Eugnostos the Blessed was written to a Gnostic audience that may not have been Christian, whereas *The Sophia of Jesus Christ* was written to Christian Gnostics or the Gnostics the writer wished to sway toward Gnostic Christianity. One of the modes of persuasion was to place the words from *Eugnostos the Blessed* on the lips of Jesus in a dialog explaining the nature of God and the heavenly creations. The Gnostic cosmology, (as well as the path and plan of divine power and manifestation), is complex and deserves explanation in order to better understand the texts of *Eugnostos the Blessed* and *The Sophia of Jesus Christ*.

First, let us look at some simple definitions.

The Sophia of Jesus and Eugnostos the Blessed

"**Gnosticism**: A system of religion mixed with Greek and Oriental philosophy of the 1st through 6th centuries A.D. Intermediate between Christianity and paganism, Gnosticism taught that knowledge rather than faith was the greatest good and that through knowledge alone could salvation be attained."

> Webster's Dictionary

Tractate | ˈtrakˌtāt |
noun formal
a treatise.
• a book of the Talmud.
ORIGIN late 15th cent.: from Latin tractatus, from tractare 'to handle,' frequentative of trahere.

> Dictionary - Apple Inc.

"**Sophia** (σοφία, Greek for "wisdom") is a central idea in Hellenistic philosophy and religion, Platonism, Gnosticism, Orthodox Christianity, Esoteric Christianity, as well as Christian mysticism. Sophiology is a philosophical concept regarding wisdom, as well as a theological concept regarding the wisdom of the biblical God.

Sophia is honored as a goddess of wisdom by Gnostics, as well as by some Neo-pagan, New Age, and feminist-inspired Goddess spirituality groups. In Orthodox and Roman Catholic Christianity, Sophia, or rather Hagia Sophia (Holy Wisdom), is an expression of understanding for the second person of the Holy Trinity, (as in the dedication of the church of Hagia Sophia in Istanbul) as well as in the Old Testament, as seen in the Book of Proverbs 9:1, but not an angel or goddess.

Sophia (Greek Σοφία, meaning "wisdom," Coptic τϲοφια tsophia) is a major theme, along with Knowledge (Greek γνῶσις gnosis, Coptic sooun), among many of the early Christian knowledge-theologies grouped by the heresiologist Irenaeus as gnostikos, "learned." Gnosticism is a 17th-century term expanding the definition of Irenaeus' groups to include other syncretic and mystery religions.

In Gnostic tradition, Sophia is a feminine figure, analogous to the human soul but also simultaneously one of the feminine aspects of God. Gnostics held that she was the syzygy of Jesus Christ (i.e. the Bride of Christ), and Holy Spirit of the Trinity. She is occasionally referred to by the Hebrew equivalent of Achamōth (Ἀχαμώθ, Hebrew חכמה chokhmah) and as Prunikos (Προύνικος). In the Nag Hammadi texts, Sophia is the lowest Aeon, or anthropic expression of the emanation of the light of God. She is considered to have fallen from grace when she created another being of some kind, without God's approval, in so doing creating or helping to create the material world."
                Wikipedia 2014

The word Gnostic is based on the Greek word "Gnosis," which means "knowledge." The "Gnosis" is the knowledge of the ultimate, supreme God and his spirit, which is contained within us all. It is this knowledge that allows one to transcend this material world with its falsities and spiritual entrapments and ascend into heaven to be one with God.

For centuries the definition of Gnosticism has in itself been a point of confusion and contention within the religious community. This is due in part to the ever-broadening application of the term and the fact that various sects of Gnosticism existed as the theology evolved and began to merge into what became mainstream Christianity.

Even though Gnosticism continued to evolve, it is the theology in place at the time that the Gnostic Gospels were written that should be considered and understood before attempting to render or read a translation. To do otherwise would make the translation cloudy and obtuse.

It becomes the duty of both translator and reader to understand the ideas being espoused and the terms conveying those ideas. A grasp of theology, cosmology, and relevant terms is necessary for a clear transmission of the meaning within the text in question.

With this in mind, we will briefly examine Gnostic theology, cosmology, and history. We will focus primarily on Gnostic sects existing in the first through fourth centuries A.D. since it is believed most Gnostic Gospels were written during that time. It was also during that time that reactions within the emerging Christian orthodoxy began to intensify.

The downfall of many books written on the topic of religion is the attempt to somehow remove history and people from the equation. History shapes religion because it shapes the perception and direction of religious leaders. Religion also develops and evolves in an attempt to make sense of the universe as it is seen and understood at the time. Thus, to truly grasp a religious concept it is important to know the history, people, and cosmology of the time. These areas are not separate but are continually interacting. This is how the information in this book will be presented to the reader.

The translations of The Sophia of Jesus Christ and Eugnostos the Blessed presented in this volume are loosely based on the work of Douglas M. Parrott, who has done extensive scholarly work on both texts. It was thought Parrott's work may appeal to highly trained theologians but was not suitable for the general public due to a style of translation which assumed a deeper knowledge of various forms of Gnosticism, as well as obscure terms and theologies. The translation herein attempts to be more clear, self-explanatory and, when needed, elucidated through commentary.

A Brief Lesson in Gnosticism

The roots of Gnosticism may pre-date Christianity. Similarities exist between Gnosticism and the wisdom and mystery cults found in Egypt and Greece. Gnosticism contains the basic terms and motifs of Plato's cosmology as well as the mystical qualities of Buddhism. Plato was steeped in Greek mythology, and the Gnostic creation myth has elements owing to this. Both cosmology and mysticism within Gnosticism present an interpretation of Christ's existence and teachings, thus, Gnostics are considered to be a Christian sect. Gnostic followers are urged to look within themselves for the truth and the Christ spirit hidden, asleep in their souls.

The battle cry can be summed up in the words of the Gnostic Gospel of Thomas, verse 3:

Jesus said: If those who lead you say to you: Look, the Kingdom is in the sky, then the birds of the sky would enter before you. If they say to you: It is in the sea, then the fish of the sea would enter ahead of you. But the Kingdom of God exists within you and it exists outside of you. Those who come to know (recognize) themselves will find it, and when you come to know yourselves you will become known and you will realize that you are the children of the Living Father. Yet if you do not come to know yourselves then you will dwell in poverty and it will be you who are that poverty.

Paganism was a religious traditional society in the Mediterranean leading up to the time of the Gnostics. Centuries after the conversion of Constantine, mystery cults worshipping various Egyptian and Greco-Roman gods continued. These cults taught that through their secret knowledge worshippers could control or escape the mortal realm. The Gnostic doctrine of inner knowledge and freedom may have part of its roots here. The concept of duality and inner guidance taught in Buddhism added to and enforced Gnostic beliefs, as we will see later.

The belief systems of Plato, Buddha, and paganism melted together, spread, and found a suitable home in the mystical side of the Christian faith as it sought to adapt and adopt certain Judeo-Christian beliefs and symbols.

Like modern Christianity, Gnosticism had various points of view that could be likened to Christian denominations of today. Complex and elaborate creation myths took root in Gnosticism, being derived from those of Plato. Later, the theology evolved and Gnosticism began to shed some of its more unorthodox myths, leaving the central theme of inner knowledge or gnosis to propagate.

The existence of various sects of Gnosticism, differing creation stories, along with the lack of historical documentation, has left scholars in a quandary about exactly what Gnostics believed. Some have suggested that the Gnostics represented a free thinking and idealistic movement much like that of the "Hippie" movement active in the United States during the 1960's.

Just as the "Hippie" movement in the U.S. influenced political thought, some early sects of Gnostics began to exert direct influence on the Christian church and its leadership.

Although it appears that there were several sects of Gnosticism, we will attempt to discuss the more universal Gnostic beliefs along with the highlights of the major sects.

Gnostic cosmology, (which is the theory of how the universe is created, constructed, and sustained), is complex and very different from orthodox Christian cosmology. In many ways Gnosticism may appear to be polytheistic or even pantheistic.

To understand some of the basic beliefs of Gnosticism, let us start with the common ground shared between Gnosticism and modern Christianity. Both believe the world is imperfect, corrupt, and brutal. The blame for this, according to mainstream Christianity, is placed squarely on the shoulders of man himself. With the fall of man (Adam), the world was forever changed to the undesirable and harmful place in which we live today. However, Gnostics reject this view as an incorrect interpretation of the creation myth.

According to Gnostics, the blame is not in ourselves, but in our creator. The creator of this world was himself somewhat less than perfect and in fact, deeply flawed and cruel, making mankind the child of a lesser God. It is in the book, *The Apocryphon of John*, that the Gnostic view of creation is presented to us in great detail.

Gnosticism also teaches that in the beginning a Supreme Being called The Father, The Divine All, The Origin, The Supreme God, or The Fullness, emanated the element of existence, both visible and invisible. His intent was not to create but, just as light emanates from a flame, so did creation shine forth from God. This manifested the primal element needed for creation. This was the creation of Barbelo, who is the Thought of God.

The Father's thought performed a deed and she was created from it. It is she who had appeared before him in the shining of his light. This is the first power which was before all of them and which was created from his mind. She is the Thought of the All and her light shines like his light. It is the perfect power which is the visage of the invisible. She is the pure, undefiled Spirit who is perfect. She is the first power, the glory of Barbelo, the perfect glory of the kingdom (kingdoms), the glory revealed. She glorified the pure, undefiled Spirit and it was she who praised him, because thanks to him she had come forth.
The Apocryphon of John

It could be said that Barbelo is the creative emanation and, like the Divine All, is both male and female. It is the "agreement" of Barbelo and the Divine All, representing the union of male and female, that created the Christ Spirit and all the Aeons. In some renderings the word "Aeon" is used to designate an ethereal realm or kingdom. In other versions "Aeon" indicates the ruler of the realm. One of these rulers was called Sophia or Wisdom. Her fall began a chain of events that led to the introduction of evil into the universe.

Seeing the Divine flame of God, Sophia sought to know its origin. She sought to know the very nature of God. Sophia's passion ended in tragedy when she managed to capture a divine and creative spark, which she attempted to duplicate with her own creative force, without the union of a male counterpart. It was this act that produced the Archons, beings born outside the higher divine realm. In the development of the myth, explanations seem to point to the fact that Sophia carried the divine essence of creation from God within her but chose to attempt creation by using her own powers. It is unclear if this was in an attempt to understand the Supreme God and his power, or an impetuous act that caused evil to enter the cosmos in the form of her creations.

The realm containing the Fullness of the Godhead and Sophia is called the pleroma or Realm of Fullness. This is the Gnostic heaven. The lesser Gods created in Sophia's failed attempt were cast outside the pleroma and away from the presence of God. In essence, she threw away and discarded her flawed creations.

"She cast it away from her, outside the place where no one of the immortals might see it, for she had created it in ignorance. And she surrounded it with a glowing cloud, and she put a throne in the middle of the cloud so that no one could see it except the Holy Spirit who is called the mother of all that has life. And she called his name Yaldaboth." Apocryphon of John

The beings Sophia created were imperfect and oblivious to the Supreme God. Her creations contained deities even less perfect than herself. They were called the Powers, the Rulers, or the Archons. Their leader was called the Demiurge, but his name was Yaldaboth. It was the flawed, imperfect, spiritually blind Demiurge, (Yaldaboth), who became the creator of the material world and all things in it. Gnostics considered Yaldaboth to be the same as Jehovah (Yahweh), who is the Jewish creator God. These beings, the Demiurge and the Archons, would later equate to Satan and his demons, or Jehovah and his angels, depending on which Gnostic sect is telling the story. Both are equally evil.

In one Gnostic creation story, the Archons created Adam but could not bring him to life. In other stories Adam was formed as a type of worm, unable to attain personhood. Thus, man began as an incomplete creation of a flawed, spiritually blind, and malevolent god. In this myth, the Archons were afraid that Adam might be more powerful than the Archons themselves. When they saw Adam was incapable of attaining the human state, their fears were put to rest, thus, they called that day the "Day of Rest."

Sophia saw Adam's horrid state and had compassion, because she knew she was the origin of the Archons and their evil. Sophia descended to help bring Adam out of his hopeless condition. It is this story that set the stage for the emergence of the sacred feminine force in Gnosticism that is not seen in orthodox Christianity. Sophia brought within herself the light and power of the Supreme God. Metaphorically, within the spiritual womb of Sophia was carried the life force of the Supreme God for Adam's salvation.

In the Gnostic text called, *The Apocryphon of John*, Sophia is quoted:
"I entered into the midst of the cage which is the prison of the body. And I spoke saying: 'He who hears, let him awake from his deep sleep.' Then Adam wept and shed tears. After he wiped away his bitter tears he asked: 'Who calls my name, and from where has this hope arisen in me even while I am in the chains of this prison?' And I (Sophia) answered: 'I am the one who carries the pure light; I am the thought of the undefiled spirit. Arise, remember, and follow your origin, which is I, and beware of the deep sleep.'"

Sophia would later equate to the Holy Spirit as the Spirit awakened the comatose soul. As the myth evolved, Sophia, after animating Adam, became Eve in order to assist Adam in finding the truth. She offered it to him in the form of the fruit of the tree of knowledge. To Gnostics, this was an act of deliverance.

Other stories have Sophia becoming the serpent in order to offer Adam a way to attain the truth. In either case, the fruit represented the hard sought truth, which was the knowledge of good and evil, and through that knowledge Adam could become a god. Later, the serpent would become a feminine symbol of wisdom, probably owing to the connection with Sophia. Eve, being Sophia in disguise, would become the mother and sacred feminine of us all. As Gnostic theology began to coalesce, Sophia would come to be considered a force or conduit of the Holy Spirit, in part due to the fact that the Holy Spirit was also considered a feminine and creative force from the Supreme God. The Gospel of Philip echoes this theology in verse six as follows:

In the days when we were Hebrews we were made orphans, having only our Mother. Yet when we believed in the Messiah (and became the ones of Christ), the Mother and Father both came to us. Gospel of Philip

As the emerging orthodox church became more and more oppressive to women, later even labeling them "occasions of sin," the Gnostics countered by raising women to equal status with men, saying Sophia was, in a sense, the handmaiden or wife of the Supreme God, making the soul of Adam her spiritual offspring.

In Gnostic cosmology the "living" world is under the control of entities called Aeons, of which Sophia is head. This means the Aeons influence or control the soul, life force, intelligence, thought, and mind. Control of the mechanical or inorganic world is given to the Archons. They rule the physical aspects of systems, regulation, limits, and order in the world. Both the ineptitude and cruelty of the Archons are reflected in the chaos and pain of the material realm.

The lesser God that created the world, Yaldaboth. began his existence in a state that was both detached and remote from the Supreme God in aspects both spiritual and physical. Since Sophia had misused her creative force, which passed from the Supreme God to her, Sophia's creation, the Demiurge, Yaldaboth, contained only part of the original creative spark of the Supreme Being. He was created with an imperfect nature caused by his distance in lineage and in spirit from the Divine All or Supreme God. It is because of his imperfections and limited abilities the lesser God is also called the "Half-Maker".

The Creator God, the Demiurge, and his helpers, the Archons took the stuff of existence produced by the Supreme God and fashioned it into this material world.

Since the Demiurge (Yaldaboth) had no memory of how he came to be alive, he did not realize he was not the true creator. The Demiurge believed he somehow came to create the material world by himself. The Supreme God allowed the Demiurge and Archons to remain deceived.

The Creator God (the Demiurge) intended the material world to be perfect and eternal, but he did not have it in himself to accomplish the feat. What comes forth from a being cannot be greater than the highest part of him, can it? The world was created flawed and transitory and we are part of it. Can we escape? The Demiurge was imperfect and evil. So was the world he created. If it was the Demiurge who created man and man is called upon to escape the Demiurge and find union with the Supreme God, is this not demanding that man becomes greater than his creator? Spiritually this seems impossible, but as many children become greater than their parents, man is expected to become greater than his maker, the Demiurge. This starts with the one fact that the Demiurge denies: the existence and supremacy of the Supreme God.

Man was created with a dual nature as the product of the material world of the Demiurge with his imperfect essence, combined with the spark of God that emanated from the Supreme God through Sophia. A version of the creation story has Sophia instructing the Demiurge to breath into Adam that spiritual power he had taken from Sophia during his creation. It was the spiritual power from Sophia that brought life to Adam.

It is this divine spark in man that calls to its source, the Supreme God, and which causes a "divine discontent," that nagging feeling that keeps us questioning if this is all there is. This spark and the feeling it gives us keeps us searching for the truth.

The Creator God sought to keep man ignorant of his defective state by keeping him enslaved to the material world. By doing so, he continued to receive man's worship and servitude. He did not wish man to recognize or gain knowledge of the true Supreme God. Since he did not know or acknowledge the Supreme God, he viewed any attempt to worship anything else as spiritual treason.

The opposition of forces set forth in the spiritual battle over the continued enslavement of man and man's spiritual freedom set up the duality of good and evil in Gnostic theology. There was a glaring difference between the orthodox Christian viewpoint and the Gnostic viewpoint. According to Gnostics, the creator of the material world was an evil entity and the Supreme God, who was his source, was the good entity. Christians quote John 1:1 "In the beginning was the Word, and the Word was with God, and the Word was God."

According to Gnostics, only through the realization of man's true state or through death can he escape captivity in the material realm. This means the idea of salvation does not deal with original sin or blood payment. Instead, it focuses on the idea of awakening to the fullness of the truth.

According to Gnostic theology, neither Jesus nor his death can save anyone, but the truth that he came to proclaim can allow a person to save his or her own soul. It is the truth, or realization of the lie of the material world and its God, that sets one on a course of freedom.

To escape the earthly prison and find one's way back to the pleroma (heaven) and the Supreme God, is the soteriology (salvation doctrine) and eschatology (judgment, reward, and doctrine of heaven) of Gnosticism.

The idea that personal revelation leads to salvation, may be what caused the mainline Christian church to declare Gnosticism a heresy. The church could better tolerate alternative theological views if the views did not undermine the authority of the church and its ability to control the people. Gnostic theology placed salvation in the hands of the individual through personal revelations and knowledge, excluding the need for the orthodox church and its clergy to grant salvation or absolution. This fact, along with the divergent interpretation of the creation story, which placed the creator God, Yaldaboth or Jehovah, as the enemy of mankind, was too much for the church to tolerate. Reaction was harsh. Gnosticism was declared to be a dangerous heresy.

Gnosticism may be considered polytheistic because it espoused many "levels" of Gods, beginning with an ultimate, unknowable, Supreme God and descending as he created Sophia, and Sophia created the Demiurge (Creator God); each becoming more inferior and limited.

There is a hint of pantheism in Gnostic theology due to the fact that creation occurs because of a deterioration of the Godhead and the dispersion of the creative essence, which eventually devolves into the creation of man.

In the end, there occurs a universal reconciliation as being after being realizes the existence of the Supreme God and renounces the material world and its inferior creator.

Combined with its Christian influences, the cosmology of the Gnostics may have borrowed from the Greek philosopher, Plato, as well as from Buddhism. There are disturbing parallels between the creation myth set forth by Plato and some of those recorded in Gnostic writings.

Plato lived from 427 to 347 B.C. He was the son of wealthy Athenians and a student of the philosopher, Socrates, and the mathematician, Pythagoras. Plato himself was the teacher of Aristotle.

In Plato's cosmology, the Demiurge is an artist who imposed form on materials that already existed. The raw materials were in a chaotic and random state. The physical world must have had visible form which was put together much like a puzzle is constructed. This later gave way to a philosophy which stated that all things in existence could be broken down into a small subset of geometric shapes.

In the tradition of Greek mythology, Plato's cosmology began with a creation story. The story was narrated by the philosopher Timaeus of Locris, a fictional character of Plato's making. In his account, nature is initiated by a creator deity, called the "Demiurge," a name which may be the Greek word for "craftsman" or "artisan" or, according to how one divides the word, it could also be translated as "half-maker."

The Demiurge sought to create the cosmos modeled on his understanding of the supreme and original truth. In this way he created the visible universe based on invisible truths. He set in place rules of process such as birth, growth, change, death, and dissolution. This was Plato's "Realm of Becoming." It was his Genesis. Plato stated that the internal structure of the cosmos had innate intelligence and was therefore called the World Soul. The cosmic super-structure of the Demiurge was used as the framework on which to hang or fill in the details and parts of the universe. The Demiurge then appointed his underlings to fill in the details which allowed the universe to remain in a working and balanced state. All phenomena of nature resulted from an interaction and interplay of the two forces of reason and necessity.

Plato represented reason as constituting the World Soul. The material world was a necessity in which reason acted out its will in the physical realm. The duality between the will, mind, or reason of the World Soul and the material universe and its inherent flaws set in play the duality of Plato's world and is seen reflected in the beliefs of the Gnostics.

In Plato's world, the human soul was immortal, each soul was assigned to a star. Souls that were just or good were permitted to return to their stars upon their death. Unjust souls were reincarnated to try again. Escape of the soul to the freedom of the stars and out of the cycle of reincarnation was best accomplished by following the reason and goodness of the World Soul and not the physical world, which was set in place only as a necessity to manifest the patterns of the World Soul.

Although in Plato's cosmology the Demiurge was not seen as evil, in Gnostic cosmology he was considered not only to be flawed and evil, he was also the beginning of all evil in the material universe, having created it to reflect his own malice.

Following the path of Plato's cosmology, some Gnostics left open the possibility of reincarnation if the person had not reached the truth before his death.

This idea appears to be of Buddhists origin. Resurrection was a Jewish and Christian concept, which shows up in surprising ways, such as when the people asked John the Baptist if he was Elijah.
New International Version
John 1:21
They asked him, "Then who are you? Are you Elijah?" He said, "I am not." "Are you the Prophet?" He answered, "No."

Even though the Jews expected the return of Elijah, they did not look for a reincarnated prophet, but someone God would send back from paradise to earth with a perfected body through the same reanimation used to bring Jesus back to life. Reincarnation assumes a person's spirit will inhabit another body from birth. There was a possible transmission of Buddhist ideas early in the first century.

In the year 13 A.D. Roman annals record the visit of an Indian king named Pandya or Porus. He came to see Caesar Augustus carrying a letter of introduction in Greek. He was accompanied by a monk who burned himself alive in the city of Athens to prove his faith in Buddhism. The event was described by Nicolaus of Damascus as, not surprisingly, causing a great stir among the people. It is thought that this was the first transmission of Buddhist teaching to the masses.

In the second century A.D., Clement of Alexandria wrote about Buddha: "Among the Indians are those philosophers also who follow the precepts of Boutta (Buddha), whom they honour as a god on account of his extraordinary sanctity." (Clement of Alexandria, "The Stromata, or Miscellanies" Book I, Chapter XV).
"Thus philosophy, a thing of the highest utility, flourished in antiquity among the barbarians, shedding its light over the nations. And afterwards it came to Greece." (Clement of Alexandria, "The Stromata, or Miscellanies").

The Sophia of Jesus and Eugnostos the Blessed

To clarify what "philosophy" was transmitted from India to Greece, we turn to the historians Hippolytus and Epiphanius who wrote of Scythianus, "a man who had visited India around 50 A.D. They report; 'He brought 'the doctrine of the Two Principles.'" According to these writers, Scythianus' pupil Terebinthus called himself a Buddha. Some scholars suggest it was he who traveled to the area of Babylon and transmitted his knowledge to Mani, who later founded Manichaeism.

Adding to the possibility of Eastern influence, we have accounts of the Apostle Thomas' attempt to convert the people of Asia-Minor. If the Gnostic gospel bearing his name was truly written by Thomas, it was penned after his return from India, where he also encountered the Buddhist influences.

Ancient church historians mention that Thomas preached to the Parthians in Persia, and it is said he was buried in Edessa. Fourth century chronicles attribute the evangelization of India (Asia-Minor or Central Asia) to Thomas.

The text of the Gospel of Thomas, which some believe predate the four gospels, has a very "Zen-like" or Eastern flavor.

Since it is widely held that the four gospels of Matthew, Mark, Luke, and John have a common reference in the basic text of Mark, it stands to reason that all follow the same general insight and language. If The Gospel of Thomas was written in his absence from the other apostles or if it was the first gospel written, one can assume it was written outside the influences common to the other gospels.

Although the codex found in Egypt is dated to the fourth century, the actual construction of the text of Thomas is placed by most Biblical scholars at about 70–150 A.D. Most agree the time of writing was in the second century A.D.

Following the transmission of the philosophy of "Two Principals," both Manichaeism and Gnosticism retained a dualistic viewpoint. The black-versus-white dualism of Gnosticism came to rest in the evil of the material world and its maker, versus the goodness of the freed soul and the Supreme God with whom it seeks union.

Oddly, the disdain for the material world and its Creator God drove Gnostic theology to far-flung extremes in attitude, beliefs, and actions. Gnostics idolize the serpent in the "Garden of Eden" story. After all, if your salvation hinges on secret knowledge the offer of becoming gods through the knowledge of good and evil sounds wonderful. So powerful was the draw of this "knowledge myth" to the Gnostics that the serpent became linked to Sophia by some sects. This can still be seen today in our medical and veterinarian symbols of serpents on poles, conveying the ancient meanings of knowledge and wisdom.

The Sophia of Jesus and Eugnostos the Blessed

Genesis 3 (King James Version)

1 Now the serpent was more subtil than any beast of the field which the LORD God had made. And he said unto the woman, Yea, hath God said, Ye shall not eat of every tree of the garden?

2 And the woman said unto the serpent, We may eat of the fruit of the trees of the garden:

3 But of the fruit of the tree which is in the midst of the garden, God hath said, Ye shall not eat of it, neither shall ye touch it, lest ye die.

4 And the serpent said unto the woman, Ye shall not surely die:

5 For God doth know that in the day ye eat thereof, then your eyes shall be opened, and ye shall be as Gods, knowing good and evil.

It is because of their vehement struggle against the Creator God and the search for some transcendent truth, that Gnostics held the people of Sodom in high regard. The people of Sodom sought to "corrupt" the messengers sent by their enemy, the Creator God. Anything done to thwart the Demiurge and his minions was considered valiant.

Genesis 19 (King James Version)

1 And there came two angels to Sodom at even; and Lot sat in the gate of Sodom: and Lot seeing them rose up to meet them; and he bowed himself with his face toward the ground;

2 And he said, Behold now, my lords, turn in, I pray you, into your servant's house, and tarry all night, and wash your feet, and ye shall rise up early, and go on your ways. And they said, Nay; but we will abide in the street all night.

3 And he pressed upon them greatly; and they turned in unto him, and entered into his house; and he made them a feast, and did bake unleavened bread, and they did eat.

4 But before they lay down, the men of the city, even the men of Sodom, compassed the house round, both old and young, all the people from every quarter:

5 And they called unto Lot, and said unto him, Where are the men which came in to thee this night? bring them out unto us, that we may know them.

6 And Lot went out at the door unto them, and shut the door after him,

7 And said, I pray you, brethren, do not so wickedly.

8 Behold now, I have two daughters which have not known man; let me, I pray you, bring them out unto you, and do ye to them as is good in your eyes: only unto these men do nothing; for therefore came they under the shadow of my roof.

9 And they said, Stand back. And they said again, This one fellow came in to sojourn, and he will needs be a judge: now will we deal worse with thee, than with them. And they pressed sore upon the man, even Lot, and came near to break the door.

10 But the men put forth their hand, and pulled Lot into the house to them, and shut to the door.

To modern Christians, the idea of admiring the serpent, which we believe was Satan, may seem unthinkable. Supporting the idea of attacking and molesting the angels sent to Sodom to warn of the coming destruction seems appalling; but to Gnostics the real evil was the malevolent entity, the Creator God of this world. To destroy his messengers, as was the case in Sodom, would impede his mission. To obtain knowledge of good and evil, as was offered by the serpent in the garden, would set the captives free.

To awaken the inner knowledge of the true God was the battle. The material world was designed to prevent the awakening by entrapping, confusing, and distracting the spirit of man. The aim of Gnosticism was the spiritual awakening and freedom of man.

Gnostics, in the age of the early church, would preach to converts (novices) about this awakening, saying the novice must awaken the God within himself and see the trap that was the material world. Salvation came from the recognition or knowledge contained in this spiritual awakening.

Not all people were ready or willing to accept the Gnosis. Many were bound to the material world and were satisfied to be only as and where they were. These have mistaken the Creator God for the Supreme God and do not know there is anything beyond the Creator God or the material existence. These people know only the lower or earthly wisdom and not the higher wisdom above the Creator God. They were referred to as "dead."

Gnostic sects split primarily into two categories. Both branches held that those who were truly enlightened could no longer be influenced by the material world. Both divisions of Gnosticism believed that their spiritual journey could not be impeded by the material realm since the two were not only separate but in opposition. Such an attitude influenced some Gnostics toward Stoicism, choosing to abstain from the world, and others toward Epicureanism, choosing to indulge.

Major schools fell into two categories; those who rejected the material world of the Creator God, and those who rejected the laws of the Creator God. For those who rejected the world the Creator God had spawned, overcoming the material world was accomplished by partaking of as little of the world and its pleasures as possible. These followers lived very stark and ascetic lives, abstaining from meat, sex, marriage, and all things that would entice them to remain in the material realm. Other schools believed it was their duty to simply defy the Creator God and all laws that he had proclaimed. Since the Creator God had been identified as Jehovah, God of the Jews, these followers set about to break every law held dear by Christians and Jews.

As human nature is predisposed to do, many Gnostics took up the more wanton practices, believing that nothing done in their earthly bodies would affect their spiritual lives. Whether it was excesses in sex, alcohol, food, or any other assorted debaucheries, the Gnostics were safe within their faith, believing nothing spiritually bad could come of their earthly adventures.

The actions of the Gnostics are mentioned by early Church leaders. One infamous Gnostic school is actually mentioned in the Bible, as we will read later.

The world was out of balance, inferior, and corrupt. The spirit was perfect and intact. It was up to the Gnostics to tell the story, explain the error, and awaken the world to the light of truth. The Supreme God had provided a vehicle to help in their effort. He had created a teacher of light and truth.

Since the time of Sophia's mistaken creation of the Archons, there was an imbalance in the cosmos. The Supreme God began to re-establish the balance by producing Christ to teach and save man. That left only Sophia, now in a fallen and bound state, along with the Demiurge, and the Archons to upset the cosmic equation. In this theology one might loosely equate the Supreme God to the New Testament Christian God, Demiurge to Satan, the Archons to demons, the pleroma to heaven, and Sophia to the creative or regenerative force of the Holy Spirit. This holds up well except for one huge problem. If the Jews believed that Jehovah created all things, and the Gnostic believed that the Demiurge created all things, then to the Gnostic mind, the Demiurge must be Old Testament god, Jehovah, and that made Jehovah their enemy.

For those who seek that which is beyond the material world and its flawed creator, the Supreme God has sent Messengers of Light to awaken the divine spark of the Supreme God within us. This part of us will call to the True God as deep calls to deep. The greatest and most perfect Messenger of Light was the Christ. He is also referred to as The Good, Christ, Messiah, and The Word. He came to reveal the Divine Light to us in the form of knowledge.

According to the Gnostics, Christ came to show us our own divine spark and to awaken us to the illusion of the material world and its flawed maker. He came to show us the way back to the divine Fullness (The Supreme God). The path to enlightenment was the knowledge sleeping within each of us. Christ came to show us the Christ spirit living in each of us. Individual ignorance or the refusal to awaken our internal divine spark was the only original sin. Christ was the only Word spoken by God that could awaken us. Christ was also the embodiment of the Word itself. He was part of the original transmission from the Supreme God that took form on the earth to awaken the soul of man so that man might search beyond the material world.

One Gnostic view of the Incarnation was "docetic," which is an early heretical position that Jesus was never actually present in the flesh, but only appeared to be human. He was a spiritual being and his human appearance was only an illusion. Of course, the title of "heretical" can only be decided by the controlling authority of the time. In this case it was the church that was about to emerge under the rule of the Emperor Constantine.

Most Gnostics held that the Christ spirit indwelt the earthly Jesus at the time of his baptism by John, at which time Jesus received the name, and thus the power, of the Lord or Supreme God.

The Christ spirit departed from Jesus' body before his death. These two viewpoints remove the idea of God sacrificing himself as an atonement for the sins of man. The idea of atonement was not necessary in Gnostic theology since it was knowledge and not sacrifice that set one free.

Since there was a distinction in Gnosticism between the man Jesus and the Light of Christ that came to reside within him, it is not contrary to Gnostic beliefs that Mary Magdalene could have been the consort and wife of Jesus. Neither would it have been blasphemous for them to have had children.

Various sects of Gnosticism stressed certain elements of their basic theology. Each had its head teachers and its special flavor of beliefs. One of the oldest types was the Syrian Gnosticism. It existed around 120 A.D. In contrast to other sects, the Syrian lacked much of the embellished mythology of Aeons, Archons, and Angels.

The fight between the Supreme God and the Creator God was not eternal, though there was strong opposition to Jehovah, the Creator God. He was considered to have been the last of the seven angels who created this world out of divine material which emanated from the Supreme God. The Demiurge attempted to create man, but only created a miserable worm which the Supreme

God had to save by giving it the spark of divine life. Thus man was born.

According to this sect, Jehovah, the Creator God, must not be worshiped. The Supreme God calls us to his service and presence through Christ his Son. They pursued only the unknowable Supreme God and sought to obey the Supreme Deity by abstaining from eating meat and from marriage and sex, and by leading an ascetic life. The symbol of Christ was the serpent, who attempted to free Adam and Eve from their ignorance and entrapment to the Creator God.

Another Gnostic school was the Hellenistic or Alexandrian School. This system absorbed the philosophy and concepts of the Greeks. They replace their Jewish or Semitic nomenclature with Greek terms and names. The cosmology and myth had grown out of proportion and appear to our eyes to be unwieldy. Yet, this school produced two great thinkers, Basilides and Valentinus. Though born at Antioch, in Syria, Basilides founded his school in Alexandria around the year A.D. 130, where it survived for several centuries.

Valentinus first taught at Alexandria and then in Rome. He established the largest Gnostic movement around A.D. 160. This movement was founded on an elaborate mythology and a system of sexual duality of male and female interplay, both in its deities and its savior.

The Sophia of Jesus and Eugnostos the Blessed

Tertullian wrote that between 135 A.D. and 160 A.D. Valentinus, a prominent Gnostic, had great influence in the Christian church. Valentinus ascended in church hierarchy and became a candidate for the office of bishop of Rome, the office that quickly evolved into that of Pope. He lost the election by a narrow margin. Even though Valentinus was outspoken about his Gnostic slant on Christianity, he was a respected member of the Christian community until his death and was probably a practicing bishop in a church of lesser status than the one in Rome.

The main platform of Gnosticism was the ability to transcend the material world through the possession of privileged and directly imparted knowledge. Following this doctrine, Valentinus claimed to have been instructed by a direct disciple of one of Jesus' apostles, a man by the name of Theodas.

Valentinus is considered by many to be the father of modern Gnosticism. His vision of the faith is summarized by G.R.S. Mead in the book "Fragments of a Faith Forgotten."

"The Gnosis in his hands is trying to embrace everything, even the most dogmatic formulation of the traditions of the Master. The great popular movement and its incomprehensibilities were recognized by Valentinus as an integral part of the mighty outpouring; he laboured to weave all together, external and internal, into one piece, devoted his life to the task, and doubtless only at his death perceived that for that age he was attempting the impossible. None but the very few could ever appreciate the ideal of the man, much less understand it. " (Fragments of a Faith Forgotten, p. 297)

Gnostic theology seemed to vacillate from polytheism to pantheism to dualism to monotheism, depending on the teacher and how he viewed and stressed certain areas of their creation myths. Marcion, a Gnostic teacher, espoused differences between the God of the New Testament and the God of the Old Testament, claiming they were two separate entities. According to Marcion, the New Testament God was a good true God while the Old Testament God was an evil angel. Although this may be a heresy, it pulled his school back into monotheism. The church, however, disowned him.

Syneros and Prepon, disciples of Marcion, postulated three different entities, carrying their teachings from monotheism into polytheism in one stroke. In their system the opponent of the good God was not the God of the Jews, but Eternal Matter, which was the source of all evil. Matter, in this system became a principal creative force. Although it was created imperfect, it could also create, having the innate intelligence of the "world soul."

Of all the Gnostic schools or sects the most famous is the Antinomian School. Believing that the Creator God, Jehovah, was evil, they sat out to disrupt all things connected to the Jewish God. This included his laws. It was considered their duty to break any law of morality, diet, or conduct given by the Jewish God, who they considered the evil Creator God. The leader of the sect was called

The Sophia of Jesus and Eugnostos the Blessed

Nicolaites. The sect existed in Apostolic times and is mentioned in the Bible.

Revelation 2 (King James Version)
5 Remember therefore from whence thou art fallen, and repent, and do the first works; or else I will come unto thee quickly, and will remove thy candlestick out of his place, except thou repent.
6 But this thou hast, that thou hatest the deeds of the Nicolaitanes, which I also hate.

Revelation 2 (King James Version)
14 But I have a few things against thee, because thou hast there them that hold the doctrine of Balaam, who taught Balac to cast a stumbling block before the children of Israel, to eat things sacrificed unto idols, and to commit fornication.
15 So hast thou also them that hold the doctrine of the Nicolaitanes, which thing I hate.
16 Repent; or else I will come unto thee quickly, and will fight against them with the sword of my mouth.

One of the leaders of the Nocolaitanes, according to Origen, was Carpocrates, whom Tertullian called a magician and a fornicator. Carpocretes taught that one could only escape the cosmic powers by discharging one's obligations to them and disregarding their laws. The Christian church fathers, St. Justin, Irenaeus, and Eusebius wrote that the reputation of these men (the Nicolaitanes), brought infamy upon the whole race of Christians.

Although Gnostic sects varied, they had certain points in common. These commonalities included salvation through special knowledge, and the fact that the world was corrupt as it was created by an evil God.

According to Gnostic theology, nothing can come from the material world that is not flawed. Because of this, Gnostics did not believe that Christ could have been a corporeal being. Thus, there must be some separation or distinction between Jesus, as a man, and Christ, as a spiritual being born from the Supreme, unrevealed, and eternal God.

To closer examine this theology, we turn to Valentinus, the driving force of early Gnosticism, for an explanation. Valentinus divided Jesus Christ into two very distinct parts; Jesus, the man, and Christ, the anointed spiritual messenger of God. These two forces met in the moment of Baptism when the Spirit of God came to rest on Jesus and the Christ power entered his body.

Here Gnosticism runs aground on its own theology, for if the spiritual cannot mingle with the material then how can the Christ spirit inhabit a body? The result of the dichotomy was a schism within Gnosticism. Some held to the belief that the specter of Jesus was simply an illusion produced by Christ himself to enable him to do his work on earth. It was not real, not matter, not corporeal, and did not actually exist as a physical body would. Others came to believe that Jesus must have been a specially prepared vessel and was the perfect human body formed by the very essence of the plumora (heaven). It was this path of thought that allowed Jesus to continue as human, lover, and father.

Jesus, the man, became a vessel containing the Light of God, called Christ. In the Gnostic view we all could and should become Christs, carrying the Truth and Light of God. We are all potential vehicles of the same Spirit that Jesus held within him when he was awakened to the Truth.

The suffering and death of Jesus then took on much less importance in the Gnostic view, as Jesus was simply part of the corrupt world and was suffering the indignities of this world as any man would. Therefore, from their viewpoint, he could have been married and been a father without disturbing Gnostic theology in the least.

The Gnostic texts seem to divide man into parts, although at times the divisions are somewhat unclear. The divisions alluded to may include the soul, which is the will of man; the spirit, which is depicted as wind or air (pneuma) and contains the holy spark that is the spirit of God in man; and the material human form, the body. The mind of man sits as a mediator between the soul, or will, and the spirit, which is connected to God.

Without the light of the truth, the spirit is held captive by the Demiurge, which enslaves man. This entrapment is called "sickness." It is this sickness that the Light came to heal and then to set us free. The third part of man, his material form, was considered a weight, an anchor, and a hindrance, keeping man attached to the corrupted earthly realm.

As we read the text, we must realize that Gnosticism conflicted with traditional Christianity. Overall theology can rise and fall upon small words and terms. If Jesus was not God, his death and thus his atonement meant nothing. His suffering meant nothing. Even the resurrection meant nothing, if one's view of Jesus was that he was not human to begin with, as was true with some Gnostics.

For the Gnostics, resurrection of the dead was unthinkable since flesh as well as all matter is destined to perish. According to Gnostic theology, there was no resurrection of the flesh, but only of the soul. How the soul would be resurrected was explained differently by various Gnostic groups, but all denied the resurrection of the body. To the enlightened Gnostic the actual person was the spirit who used the body as an instrument to survive in the material world but did not identify with it. This belief is echoed in the Gospel of Thomas.

29. Jesus said: If the flesh came into being because of spirit, it is a marvel, but if spirit came into being because of the body, it would be a marvel of marvels. I marvel indeed at how great wealth has taken up residence in this poverty.

The Sophia of Jesus and Eugnostos the Blessed

Owing to the Gnostic belief of such a separation of spirit and body, it was thought that the Christ spirit within the body of Jesus departed the body before the crucifixion. Others said the body was an illusion and the crucifixion was a sham perpetrated by an eternal spirit on the men that sought to kill it. Lastly, some suggested that Jesus deceived the soldiers into thinking he was dead. The resurrection under this circumstance became a lie which allowed Jesus to escape and live on in anonymity, hiding, living as a married man, and raising a family until his natural death.

Think of the implications to the orthodox Christian world if the spirit of God departed from Jesus as it fled and laughed as the body was crucified. This is the implication of the Gnostic interpretation of the death of Jesus when he cries out, "My power, my power, why have you left me," as the Christ spirit left his body before his death. What are the ramifications to the modern Christian if the Creator God, the Demiurge, is more evil than his creation? Can a Creation rise above its creator? Is it possible for man to find the spark within himself that calls to the Supreme God and free himself of his evil creator?

Although, in time, the creation myth and other Gnostic differences began to be swept under the rug, it was the division between Jesus and the Christ spirit that put them at odds with the emerging orthodox church. At the establishment of the doctrine of the trinity, the mainline church firmly set a divide between themselves and the Gnostics.

To this day there is a battle raging in the Christian world as believers and seekers attempt to reconcile today's Christianity to the sect of the early Christian church called, "Gnosticism."

Feminine Forces in the Old Testament

According to the Old Testament book of Genesis in the Hebrew text, there was a balance of male and female forces within God from the beginning. Neither male nor female, both male and female, God showed the male energy of forming and shaping, as well as the female energy of nurturing and brooding. Although one may have a difficult time in distinguishing God the Spirit from the Spirit of God, the word for "spirit" is "ruach" and is a female word.

Genesis 1

Amplified Bible

1) In the beginning God (prepared, formed, fashioned, and) created the heavens and the earth.

2) The earth was without form and an empty waste, and darkness was upon the face of the very great deep. The Spirit of God was moving (hovering, brooding) over the face of the waters.

The Holy Spirit is the designated representation of the feminine principle. This idea is supported by the Hebrew word for "spirit". Jerome, the author of the Latin Vulgate knew this when he rendered the passage into Latin. He is quoted as saying:

The Sophia of Jesus and Eugnostos the Blessed

"In the Gospel of the Hebrews that the Nazarenes read it says, 'Just now my mother, the Holy Spirit, took me.' Now, no one should be offended by this, because "spirit" in Hebrew is feminine, while in our language [Latin] it is masculine, and in Greek it is neuter. In divinity, however, there is no gender."

In Jerome's Commentary on Isaiah 11, an explanation contains a pointed observation. There was a tradition among a sect of Early Christians which believed that the Holy Spirit was our Lord's spiritual mother. Jerome comments that the Hebrew word for "spirit" (ruach or ruak) is feminine, meaning, that for the 1st Century Christians in the Aramaic world, the Holy Spirit was a feminine figure. This was likely because in the beginning, the converts to this new cult of Judaism, called Christianity, were mostly Jews. The gender was lost in the translation from the Hebrew into the Greek, rendering it neuter, and then it was changed to a masculine gender when it was translated from the Greek into the Latin.

The Bible in Genesis describes a male/female God with male creating and female brooding. But, man could not hold onto that unfamiliar concept and the primitive Jews chose to take up the Canaanite deities of the God, El and his wife, Asherah. But, she was simply a fertility goddess.

Although the balance of male and female energies were presented in Genesis from the outset, primitive man was not ready to accept or understand the spiritual truth of balance. Instead, mankind had to evolve spiritually over thousands of years until they were ready to resume the search for the Sacred Feminine. This time, it was within their one true God. Monotheism does not easily reveal the dualism of male and female forces.

Even today, the churches continue to struggle with the fact that God is at once male and female. God is neither. God is both. God is all.

Possibly, if we better understood the original language and context of the time, the church would not have gone so far astray. The word used for the station of women in conjunction with men is "helpmeet."

The truth has been there in the Bible all along. Let us look closely at the words used regarding the place of woman in regards to man. The word used is "Helpmeet."

HELP

Strong's # 5828 (**Hebrew - ezer**) aid: - help
Strong's Root # 5826 (Hebrew - azar) azar - prime root: to surround, i.e., protect or aid: help, succor
Heinrich Friedrich Wilhelm Gesenius (1786–1842), noted author of the first Hebrew lexicon, adds that the primary idea lies in girding, surrounding, hence defending .

MEET

(**Hebrew** - *kenegdo*) corresponding to, counterpart to, equal to, matching

The traditional teaching for the woman as help (meet) is that of assistant or helper, subservient to the one being helped. This definition would appear to line up with Strong's definition of the word. However, if you look at the context of every other use of the word *ezer* in the scripture, you will see that *ezer* refers to either God or military allies. In all other cases the one giving the help is superior to the one receiving the help. Adding *kenegdo* (meet) modifies the meaning to that of equal rather than superior status. Let us remember that it was the man was the one who needed help.

Dr. Susan Hyatt gives the following definition from her book *In the Spirit We're Equal*: "Re: Hebrew *ezer kenegdo*. In Genesis 2:18, the word "Helpmeet" does not occur. The Hebrew expression *ezer kenegdo* appears meaning, "one who is the same as the other and who surrounds, protects, aids, helps, supports." There is no indication of inferiority or of a secondary position in a hierarchical separation of the male and female "spheres" of responsibility, authority, or social position.

The word *ezer* is used twice in the Old Testament to refer to the female and 14 times to refer to God. For example, in the Psalms when David says, "The Lord is my Helper," he uses the word *ezer*." Usages of '*ezer* in the Old Testament show that in most cases God is an 'ezer to human beings, which calls to question if the word "helper" is a valid interpretation of '*ezer* in any instance it is used. "Evidence indicates that the word '*ezer* originally had two roots, each beginning with different guttural sounds. One meant "power" and the other "strength." As time passed, the two guttural sounds merged, but the meanings remained the same. The article below by William Sulik explains this point quite well. He references R. David Freedman and Biblical Archaeology   Review 9 [1983]: (56-58).

"She was to be his "helper". At least, that is how most of the translations have interpreted this word. A sample of the translations reads as follows:
'I shall make a helper fit for him' (RSV); 'I will make a fitting helper for him' (New Jewish Publication Society); 'I will make an aid fit for him' (AB); 'I will make him a helpmate' (JB); 'I will make a suitable partner for him' (NAB); 'I will make him a helper comparable to him' (NKJV).

[Source: *Hard Sayings of the Bible* by Walter C. Kaiser, Peter H. Davids, F. F. Bruce, and Manfred Brauch]

However, the customary translation of the two words `*ezer kenegdo* as "helper fit" is almost certainly wrong. Recently R. David

The Sophia of Jesus and Eugnostos the Blessed

Freedman has pointed out that the Hebrew word *ezer* is a combination of two roots: `-z-r, meaning "to rescue, to save," and g-z-r, meaning "to be strong." The difference between the two is the first letter in the Hebrew language.

Today, that letter is silent in the Hebrew; but in ancient times, it was a guttural sound formed in the back of the throat. The "g" was a *ghayyin*, and it came to use the same Hebrew symbol as the other sound, `ayin. But the fact that they were pronounced differently is clear from such names of places which preserve the "g" sound, such as Gaza or Gomorrah. Some Semitic languages distinguished between these two signs and others did not. For example, Ugaritic did make a distinction between the `ayin and the *ghayyin*; Hebrew did not. (R. David Freedman, "*Woman, a Power Equal to a Man,*" Biblical Archaeology Review 9 [1983]: 56-58).

It would appear that sometime around 1500 BCE, these two signs began to be represented by one sign in Phoenician. Consequently, the two "phonemes" merged into one "grapheme." What had been two different roots merged into one, much as in English the one word "fast" can refer to a person's speed, abstinence from food, his or her slyness in a "fast deal," or the adamant way in which someone holds "fast" to positions. The noun `ezer occurs twenty-one times in the Old Testament. In many of the passages, it is used in parallelism to words that clearly denote strength or power. Some examples of this are:

"There is none like the God of Jeshurun, The Rider of the Heavens in your strength (`-z-r), and on the clouds in his majesty."

(Deut.33:26 [source author's translation])

"Blessed are you, O Israel! Who is like you, a people saved by the Lord? He is the shield of your strength (`-z-r) and the sword of your majesty." (Deut. 33:29, [source author's translation]

The case begins to build for the surety that `ezer means "strength" or "power" whenever it is used in parallelism with words for majesty or other words for power such as `oz or `uzzo. In fact, the presence of two names for one king, Azariah and Uzziah, both referring to God's strength, makes it abundantly clear that the root `ezer meaning "strength" was known in Hebrew.

Therefore, we could conclude that Genesis 2:18 be translated as, "I will make a power [or strength] corresponding to man." Freedman even suggests, on the basis of later Hebrew, that the second word in the Hebrew expression found in this verse should be rendered "equal to him." If so, then God makes a woman fully his equal and fully his match for the man.

The same line of reasoning occurs with the apostle Paul, who urged in 1 Corinthians 11:10, "For this reason, a woman must have power [or authority] on her head [that is to say, invested in her]."

This line of reasoning, which stresses full equality, is continued in Genesis 2:23 where Adam says of Eve, "This is now bone of my bones and flesh of my flesh; she shall be called 'woman,' for she was taken out of man." The idiomatic sense of this phrase, "bone of my bones", is a "very close relative" to "one of us" or, in effect, "our equal."

The woman was never meant to be an assistant or "helpmate" to the man. The word "mate" slipped into English since it was so close to the Old English word "meet," which means "fit to" or "corresponding to" the man which comes from the phrase that likely means "equal to."

What God had intended, then, was to make a "power" or "strength" for the man who would in every way "correspond to him", or "be his equal." The closest word connecting the corporeal station of "helpmeet" to the spiritual world within the Godhead is the word that explains the female attributes and energies within God. That word is "Ruach," also spelled "Ruak," since transliteration from Hebrew is not precise. The spirit of God, Ruach, is a female word. Ruach broods and nurtures. She "mothers." To this day, few people, Jew or Christian, have understood this. Others continue to view the deities as two separate entities, just as Yahweh and His consort.

Let us consider a word or two and the various ways the translators have decided to render the words. We will begin with the Hebrew word, "*Chayil.*"

Virtuous = Strong's #2428 (*chayil*) wealth, virtue, valor, strength, might, power.

Before we precede, it must be understood that Hebrew has a reasonably small lexicon. Words are interpreted according to context. The same form may be used as a noun, a verb, an adjective, or an adverb.

Chayil occurs 242 times in the Old Testament. It is translated "army" and "war" 58 times; "host" and "forces" 43 times; "might" or "power" 16 times; "goods," "riches," "substance" and "wealth" in all 31 times; "band of soldiers," "band of men," "company," and "train" once each"; "activity" once; "valor" 28 times; "strength" 11 times: these are all noun forms. The word is often translated as an adjective or adverb.

It is translated "valiant" and "valiantly" 35 times; "strong" 6 times; "able" 4 times; "worthily" once, and "worthy" once. One can see a pattern to the translations of the word. All choices connote power, war, ability, and substance. However, these are the translations of the word only when the translators saw that the word applied to a male, or the actions or results of actions enacted by a man or by men.

In the four instances in which the word is used in describing a woman, the word seems to be rendered as if it were not the same word. In the four cases relating to women, the word is translated differently, and the choices of the words used to rendered *Chayil* into English shows a gender bias.

Ruth, the Moabitess, was a woman of courage, loyalty, and decisiveness. In her loyalty to her dead husband's mother, she refused to leave her mother-in-law and re-marry in her own land, but was inalterably determined to accompany her mother-in-law to a foreign land. There, in an unknown city she committed herself to the task of keeping them both from starvation. She labored tirelessly. Boaz, recognizing her traits would later say to her: "All the city of my people doth know that thou art a woman of *cha-yil*," (Ruth 3:11). The Septuagint rendered the Hebrew word, *Chayil*, into Greek as follows, "Thou art a woman of power" (dunamis).

In the last chapter of Proverbs, there is a description of an ideal wife, whose "price is far above rubies." Here are some of her characteristics: "She is like the merchants' ships, she brings her food from afar." "She considers a field and buys it." "She girds her loins with strength, and strengthens her arms." "Strength and honor are her clothing." The is obviously a woman of determination, strength, and will. This is the kind of woman a mother would choose to marry her son. The translators wrote: "Who can find a virtuous woman? "Virtue" is a moral quality, but does not capture the impressive strength of a women who works day and night in many areas of life and is a success in them all, as the Proverb indicated about this woman. The word used for "Virtue" is the Hebrew word, "*Chayil*." She is a "Mighty" woman.

The ideal woman is summed up in the 29th verse, in the words: "Many daughters have done *cha-yil*, but thou excel them all." "Worthily," "valiantly," are the only translations that we have in any other part of the Bible for this word where it is applied to a man, but here, the word is translated "virtuously" to the female. This pressed the medieval concept of sexual purity into the text where it was not necessarily intended.

In Proverbs 12:4, the Hebrew text reads, "A woman of *cha-yil* is a crown to her husband." The translators render the English text as, "A virtuous woman is a crown to her husband." Again, Septuagint translates the word as a word for strength, power, might, valor, ability, uprightness, integrity.

To sum up the difference in word choices of the translation of "*Chayil*", let us look at the grouping of the examples below:

Ruth 3:11 And now my daughter, fear not, I will do to thee all that thou require; for all the city of my people know that thou art a virtuous [*chayil*] woman.

Proverbs 12:4 A virtuous [*chayil*] woman is a crown to her husband; but she that makes ashamed is as rottenness in his bones.

The Sophia of Jesus and Eugnostos the Blessed

Proverbs 31:10 Who can find a virtuous *[chayil]* woman? For her price is far above rubies.

Proverbs 31:29 Many daughters have done virtuously *[chayil]*, but thou excel them all.

In **Ps. 18:32 and 39** the word *Chayil* is translated as strength.

Ps.18:32 It is God that girds me with strength *[chayil]*, and makes my way perfect.
vs. 39 For thou hast girded me with strength *[chayil]* unto the battle: thou hast subdued under me those that rose up against me.

The Torah Study for Reform Jews says, "From the time of creation, relationships between spouses have at times been adversarial."

In Genesis 2:18, God calls woman an *ezer kenegdo,* a "helper against him." The great commentator, Rashi, takes the term literally to make a wonderful point: "If he [Adam] is worthy, [she will be] a help *[ezer]*. If he is not worthy [she will be] against him *[kenegdo]* for strife." This Jewish study also described man and woman facing each other with arms raised holding an arch between them, giving a beautiful picture of equal responsibility.

Although a small number of Christian denominations have managed to re-capture some type of balance between male and female energy within the godhead, most have not.

An official publication of the LDS (Mormon) Church states:
"Our Father in heaven was once a man as we are now, capable of physical death. By obedience to eternal gospel principles, he progressed from one stage of life to another until he attained the state that we call exaltation or godhood. In such a condition, he and our mother in heaven were empowered to give birth to spirit children whose potential was equal to that of their heavenly parents. We are those spirit children." (Achieving a Celestial Marriage p 132)

The LDS (Mormon) Church offers courses in religion and supplies books and manuals from which to teach. In the 3rd chapter of the manual for a course entitled, *Doctrines of the Gospel,* that is part of an advanced course for the Religion 231 and 232, we find the church addresses the nature of God. Joseph Smith's "King Follett" sermon is cited as authoritative by this official Church publication along with a statement from Spencer W. Kimball, one of the earlier church prophets:

God made man in his own image and certainly he made woman in the image of his wife-partner (Spencer W. Kimball, The Teachings of Spencer W. Kimball, p.25).

Again we encounter the concept of the heavenly Mother, God's wife in heaven, and have the interesting assertion that women are made, not in the image of God, but in the image of God's wife-partner.

The Sophia of Jesus and Eugnostos the Blessed

In the above quotes, we see the Church of Jesus Christ of Latter day Saints sought to fill the void of the divine or Sacred Feminine with an entity, who was the wife of God.

It is within the Christian Science Church, also called the Church of Christ Scientists, that the balance of a singular God containing all attributes of both male and female is encountered again after thousands of years.

In the church of Christ Scientists (Christian Science), God is hailed as "The Mother-Father God," vocalizing their held belief of the existence of attributes and energies of both male and female within the spirit of God.

Mary Baker Eddy defined God as "the all-knowing, all-seeing, all-acting, all-wise, all-loving, and eternal; Principle; Mind; Soul; Spirit; Truth; Love; all substance; intelligence" (Eddy 587). Very importantly, Mrs. Eddy throughout her writing also refers to God as the Father-Mother God.

Mary Baker Eddy was not the first one to perceive God as being both Father and Mother (Peel 91). Mother Ann Lee, a Shaker woman, was part of just one of many faiths that spoke of God as Mother. She wrote:

"As Father, God is the infinite Fountain of intelligence, and the Source of all power, "the Almighty and terrible in majesty"; "the high and lofty one, that inhabiteth eternity, whose name is Holy, dwelling in the high and holy

place"; and "a consuming fire." But as, Mother, "God is Love" and tenderness. If all the maternal affections of all the female or bearing spirits in animated nature were combined together, and then concentrated in one individual human female, that person would be put as the type or image of our Eternal Heavenly Mother." (Peel 28).

This matches the Christian Science understanding of God's motherly aspects and serves as a helpful illustration of the maternal nature of God as Mother. God as Father is a powerful being that offers intelligence and strength; yet there is something untouchable about Him. God as Mother can be seen as our earthly mothers, tender, nurturing, maternal, and approachable, although it must be stated that neither "ezer" or "chyil" convey the attitude of "motherliness" as we commonly regard it.

Mary Baker Eddy produced an interpretation of the Lord's Prayer based on her understanding of the balance of male and female elements within the Godhead.

Lord's Prayer with Spiritual Interpretation by Mary Baker Eddy
Our Father which art in heaven,
Our Father-Mother God, all-harmonious,
Hallowed be Thy name.
Adorable One.
Thy kingdom come.
Thy kingdom is come; Thou art ever-present.
Thy will be done in earth, as it is in heaven.

Enable us to know – as in heaven, so on earth – God is omnipotent, supreme.

Give us this day our daily bread;

Give us grace for today; feed the famished affections;

And forgive us our debts, as we forgive our debtors.

And Love is reflected in love;

And lead us not into temptation, but deliver us from evil;

And God leadeth us not into temptation, but delivereth us from sin, disease, and death.

For Thine is the kingdom, and the power, and the glory, forever.

For God is infinite, all-power, all Life, Truth, Love, over all, and All.

Defining The Divine Feminine

Having seen some of the attempts of the modern churches to understand and rectify the lack of recognition or understanding of the Divine Feminine, it is necessary to ask, "What happened to the Divine Feminine of Genesis? What initiated the lack of recognition or denial of the female side of God?"

The feminine side of God was erased with the change of language from the Hebrew feminine word "Ruak" into the Greek word "Pneuma" and into the Latin word "Spiritus". Both words, Spiritus and Pneuma mean "breath", but the word used in Latin is a masculine word and in Greek the word has no gender at all. Thus the feminine side of God simply disappeared into a linguistic void and was forgotten; never to be recognized for her nurturing and brooding nature until centuries later. Since the church was almost completely controlled by men at the time, they either did not notice or they did not care that the feminine spirit of God vanished and was replaced with a translation that rendered the spirit of God either neuter or masculine.

Although it is understood that God is a singular being, our psyches still call out for some manifestation of the female force. We long for a mother as well as a father. We search the Bible for the Sacred

Feminine. In its pages we find no less than three distinct feminine archetypal forms within God: Ruak, Shikina, and Sophia (Wisdom).

In the pages of the New Testament and the teaching of the Catholic Church, we find the Divine Feminine, also called the Sacred Feminine, exemplified in the persons of Mary Magdalene and Mary, the mother of Jesus.

Let us first look at the feminine forces of Ruak, Shikhinah, and Sophia (Wisdom).

Ruak, Ruach, or Rawach:
We have already seen that Ruak was the spirit that hovered and brooded over the earth like a mother hen broods over her chicks. In the Ten Commandments, we are taught to "honor your father and your mother" and that doing so would make "your days long upon the land which Yahweh your God is giving you." There seems to be no obvious connection in the temporal sense, except that by not honoring your parents you could be stoned. However, if Yahweh is actually speaking of our spiritual father and mother, that is Yahweh and His Holy Spirit, then it all makes sense. Yahweh is the Creator, Provider, Protector, and ultimate Authority. These are all "male" traits. Ruak Qodesh or Holy Spirit is the maternal aspect of God. She is the Caregiver, Counselor, and Comforter.

Shekinah, Shechinah, Shekhina, or Shechina.

Joseph Lumpkin

In the Hebrew language this word means the glory or radiance of God. The Glory of God rests or resides in his house or Tabernacle amongst his people. Thus, the word is derived from the Hebrew word 'sakan', which means 'to dwell'.

The Shekhina is defined, in traditional Jewish writings, as the "female aspect of God." It is part of the feminine "presence" of the infinite God in the world. She is introduced in early rabbinical commentaries as the "immanence" or "indwelling" of the living God. Her purpose is to animate or impart life force. She is certainly not the 'Canaanite' Mother Goddess, Asherah. Around 622 BCE, King Josiah removed the Asherah from the Jerusalem temple and destroyed the shrines.

While she does not appear by name in the five books of Moses, her presence is seen in interpreting the text. For example, when Moses encounters the burning bush, he is told to remove his shoes and prepare himself to receive the Shekhina.

A Talmudic verse said: "Let them make Me a sanctuary that I may dwell (*ve'shakhanti*) among them." In a later version, the translation said, "Let them make Me a Sanctuary so that My Shekhina will dwell among them."

A Talmudic quotation from the end of the 1st century BCE: " ...while the Children of Israel were still in Egypt, the Holy One, blessed be He, stipulated that He would liberate them from Egypt only in order that they built him a Sanctuary so that He can let His Shekhina dwell among them ... As soon as the Tabernacle was erected, the Shekhina descended and dwelt among them."

Another quotation from early 3rd century says: "On that day a thing came about which had never existed since the creation of the world. From the creation of the world and up to that hour, the Shekhina had never dwelt among the lower beings. But from the time that the Tabernacle was erected, she did dwell among them."

Although the language of the text may lead us to view "her" as a separate entity, the Shekhina is a specific way the Spirit of God is manifesting. She gives life. This is the most powerful of female attributes.

Another tradition claimed that she had always dwelt among her people, but their sins drove her, from time to time, into heaven. However, she was drawn back to her children and tried to save them, over and over. This viewpoint is more in line with the New Testament idea of the Holy Spirit.

Keeping with the idea of the Shekhina returning to the people, when the Jews were exiled to Babylonia, she transferred her seat there, and appeared alternately in two major synagogues.

Jewish tradition and teaching tells us that as the Jews dispersed throughout the world, the Shekhina comforted the poor and the suffering. She drew the sinner back to God by enlivening their spirit and conscience. She caused sinners to repent and then accepted and comforted them as if they had never sinned. Spiritually, she carried aloft the suffering and those whose hearts were broken and whose spirit was low. They were seated next to the Shekhina.. "When their spirits were healed, the Shekhina walked with them every day...."

Since we are limited in our understanding, the idea of a single entity, even a spirit, being in two places at once was disconcerting for the people. The paradox of dwelling in one place, and being other places with many people at the same time, had to be resolved.

The Talmud attempted to explain the paradox within a simple and well-known anecdote. "The Emperor said to Raban Gamaliel: 'You say that wherever ten men are assembled, the Shekhina dwells among them'."

Still, we continued to worry over the fact that God was at once in heaven and on the earth, manifesting as Shekhina. An interesting Medieval story and teaching shows the Shekhina as a total separate entity, in her most important role - interceding on behalf of her children.

Another story shows her being equated to an intercessor. "The Shekhina comes to the defense of sinful Israel by saying first to Israel: 'Be not a witness against thy neighbor without a cause' and then thereafter saying to God: 'Say not: I will do to him as he hath done to me..' "

This is obviously a conversation taking place among three distinct entities - Israel, God, and the Shekhina.

Another significant passage from the 11th century, describes Rabbi Akiva (a second century sage) saying: "When the Holy One, blessed be He, considered the deeds of the generation of Enoch and that they were spoiled and evil, *He removed Himself and His Shekhina* from their midst and ascended into the heights with blasts of trumpets..."

The Talmud reports that the Shekhina is what caused prophets to prophesy and King David to compose his Psalms. The Shekhina manifests herself as a form of joy, connected with prophecy and creativity. (Talmud Pesachim 117a)

The Shekhina is associated with the transformational spirit of God regarded as the source of prophecy:
"After that thou shalt come to the hill of God, where is the garrison of the Philistines; and it shall come to pass, when thou art come thither to the city, that thou shalt meet a band of prophets coming down from the high place with a psaltery, and a timbrel, and a pipe, and a harp, before them; and they will be prophesying.
And the spirit of the LORD will come mightily upon thee, and thou shalt prophesy with them, and shalt be turned into another man." (1 Samuel 10:5-6 JPS).

The 16th century mystic, Rabbi Isaac Luria, wrote a famous Shabbat hymn about the Shekhina or Glory of God. In it we see how this part of God is directly equated with a bride:

"I sing in hymns to enter the gates of the Field of holy apples.
A new table we prepare for Her, a lovely candelabrum sheds its light upon us.
Between right and left the Bride approaches, in holy jewels and festive garments..."

Zohar states: "One must prepare a comfortable seat with several cushions and embroidered covers, from all that is found in the house, like one who prepares a canopy for a bride. For the Shabbat is a queen and a bride. This is why the masters of the Mishna used to go out on the eve of Shabbat to receive her on the road, and used to say: '*Come, O bride, come, O bride!*' And one must sing and rejoice at the table in her honor ... one must receive the Lady with many lighted candles, many enjoyments, beautiful clothes, and a house embellished with many fine appointments ..."

The tradition of the Shekhina as the Shabbat Bride continues to this day as a powerful and moving symbol of the Sacred or Divine Feminine.

Wisdom or Sophia:

The Sophia of Jesus and Eugnostos the Blessed

We must also look in the Old Testament, the Hebrew Bible, and consider Sophia. Her name means "Wisdom," and she is found repeatedly in scripture as the wife or consort of God.

Proverbs 8
Wisdom's Call

1) Does not wisdom call out?
   Does not understanding raise her voice?
2) At the highest point along the way,
   where the paths meet, she takes her stand;
3) beside the gate leading into the city,
   at the entrance, she cries aloud:
4) "To you, O people, I call out;
   I raise my voice to all mankind.
5) You who are simple, gain prudence;
   you who are foolish, set your hearts on it (Wisdom).
6) Listen, for I have trustworthy things to say;
   I open my lips to speak what is right.
7) My mouth speaks what is true,
   for my lips detest wickedness.
8) All the words of my mouth are just;
   none of them are crooked or perverse.
9) To the discerning all of them are right;
   they are upright to those who have found knowledge.
10) Choose my instruction instead of silver,
    knowledge rather than choice gold,
11) for wisdom is more precious than rubies,

and nothing you desire can compare with her.

12) I, wisdom, dwell together with prudence; I possess knowledge and discretion.

13) To fear the LORD is to hate evil; I hate pride and arrogance, evil behavior and perverse speech.

14) Counsel and sound judgment are mine; I have insight, I have power.

15) By me kings reign and rulers issue decrees that are just;

16) by me princes govern, and nobles—all who rule on earth.

17) I love those who love me, and those who seek me find me.

18) With me are riches and honor, enduring wealth and prosperity.

19) My fruit is better than fine gold; what I yield surpasses choice silver.

20) I walk in the way of righteousness, along the paths of justice,

21) bestowing a rich inheritance on those who love me and making their treasuries full.

22) The LORD brought me forth as the first of his works, before his deeds of old;

23) I was formed long ages ago, at the very beginning, when the world came to be.

24) When there were no watery depths, I was given birth, when there were no springs overflowing with water;

25) before the mountains were settled in place, before the hills, I was given birth,

26) before he made the world or its fields or any of the dust of the earth.

The Sophia of Jesus and Eugnostos the Blessed

27) I was there when he set the heavens in place, when he marked out the horizon on the face of the deep,

28) when he established the clouds above and fixed securely the fountains of the deep,

29) when he gave the sea its boundary so the waters would not overstep his command, and when he marked out the foundations of the earth.

30) Then I was constantly at his side. I was filled with delight day after day, rejoicing always in his presence,

31) rejoicing in his whole world and delighting in mankind.

32) "Now then, my children, listen to me; blessed are those who keep my ways.

33) Listen to my instruction and be wise; do not disregard it.

34) Blessed are those who listen to me, watching daily at my doors, waiting at my doorway.

35) For those who find me find life and receive favor from the LORD.

36) But those who fail to find me harm themselves; all who hate me love death."

Although the mainstream Christian church would forget about Sophia, the Gnostic Christians would not. In their unorthodox theology, they fought to understand the duality of the world and the Sacred Feminine. The Gnostic movement started before second century A.D., but was condemned by the emerging powers of the orthodox church and newly established church fathers. They could not control the people through Gnostic theology, which taught there was an individual transmission of knowledge from God to the individual without the help or interference of priests or church.

Most Gnostics were suppressed or killed. The last great Gnostic movement came from the Cathars. Catharism represented total opposition to the Catholic church, which they basically viewed as a large, pompous, and fraudulent organization which had lost its integrity and "sold out" for power and money in this world, a world which the Gnostics viewed as evil.

As time went on and the mainstream church became established in its power base, they could more effectively fight their enemies. The Inquisition was proof of this.

In an attempt to cleanse the world of the Gnostics once and for all, whole villages and cities were annihilated, including women and children, and even Catholics, with the justification by the church that this serious heresy must be eliminated no matter what the consequences. Arnold Aimery, the Papal Legate at the siege of Beziers, ordered his men: "Show mercy neither to order, nor to age, nor to sex....Cathar or Catholic, Kill them all... God will know his own....".

Catharism, one of the last great sects of Gnosticism, vanished from the stage of history by the end of the 14th century due to that final, fateful siege of Monsegur in 1244.

The Sophia of Jesus and Eugnostos the Blessed

Gnostic texts were preserved and many were found in 1945 in Nag Hammadi, Egypt.

In the Gnostic text called, *The Apocryphon of John,* Sophia is quoted: *"I entered into the midst of the cage which is the prison of the body. And I spoke saying: 'He who hears, let him awake from his deep sleep.' Then Adam wept and shed tears. After he wiped away his bitter tears he asked: 'Who calls my name, and from where has this hope arose in me even while I am in the chains of this prison?' And I (Sophia) answered: 'I am the one who carries the pure light; I am the thought of the undefiled spirit. Arise, remember, and follow your origin, which is I, and beware of the deep sleep.'"*

As the myth evolved, Sophia, after animating Adam, became Eve in order to assist Adam in finding the truth. She offered it to him in the form of the fruit of the tree of knowledge. To Gnostics, this was an act of deliverance.

Other stories have Sophia becoming the serpent in order to offer Adam a way to attain the truth.
Since in the Gnostic sect of Christianity truth leads to salvation, it was Sophia, offering the knowledge of truth to Adam that symbolized salvation.

In either case, the fruit represented the hard sought truth, which was the knowledge of good and evil, and through that knowledge, Adam could become a god. Later, the serpent would become a feminine symbol of wisdom, probably owing to the connection with Sophia.

Eve, being Sophia in disguise, would become the mother and Sacred Feminine of us all. As Gnostic theology began to coalesce, Sophia would come to be considered a force or conduit of the Holy Spirit, in part due to the fact that the Holy Spirit was also considered a feminine and creative force from the Supreme God. The Gospel of Philip echoes this theology in verse six as follows:

"In the days when we were Hebrews, we were made orphans, having only our Mother. Yet when we believed in the Messiah (and became the ones of Christ), the Mother and Father both came to us. "

Sophia would later equate to the Holy Spirit as she awakened the comatose soul.

So it is that within these three: Ruak – the spirit, Shikinah – the glory, and Sophia- the wisdom, that the Sacred Feminine of God is expressed.

Understanding The Divine Feminine

A dynamic tension between the psychological need of a feminine energy, and a hesitancy to confer or concede any control to a female exists in modern Judeo-Christian religion and culture.

Carl Jung sums up the archetypes of the female as related to the stages or evolution of man's views toward women in general. To be very clear, Jung's four stages of women are the distinct stages of evolution or maturity within the male psyche and how the man views women.

Jung believed anima or life force development has four distinct levels, which he named *Eve, Helen (who we also identify with Mary Magdalene), Mary, the mother of Jesus, and Sophia or Wisdom.* In broad terms, the entire process of life force development in a male is about the male subject opening up to emotionality. In doing so, he obtains a broader spirituality by creating a new conscious paradigm that includes the intuitive processes, creativity, and imagination and psychic sensitivity towards himself and others where it might not have existed previously. Since religion is a reflection of the collective psyche, it is very important to examine these stages and how they each influence, or have influenced, religious thought in regards to women and the place of the Sacred Feminine in Christianity.

Eve

The first is *Eve*, named after the Genesis account of Adam and Eve. It deals with the emergence of a male's object of desire. This coincides with Asherah and her place as a goddess of fertility and procreation.

Helen – Mary Magdalene

The second is *Helen or Mary Magdalene.* Helen is in allusion to Helen of Troy in Greek mythology. In this phase, women are viewed as capable of worldly success and of being self-reliant, intelligent, and insightful, even if not altogether virtuous. This second phase is meant to show a strong schism in external talents (cultivated business and conventional skills) with lacking internal qualities (inability for virtue, lacking faith or imagination).
Although Mary Magdalene was not the prostitute in the biblical account, (that person was never given a name), she did have seven demons and was not considered totally virtuous, as the apostles pointed out when they sought to dissuade Jesus from being seen with her. Speculation is that Mary Magdalene was wealthy, being from a village that was know for wealthy ship owners and fishermen, and supplied funds for Jesus' ministry. Luke 8: 1-4 states plainly that Jesus was supported by women, including Mary

Magdalene, who "were helping to support Jesus and the Twelve with their own money." (NIRV)

Mary, The Mother

The third phase is *Mary*, named after the Christian theological understanding of the Virgin Mary (Jesus' mother). At this level, females can now seem to possess virtue by the perceiving male (even if in an esoteric and dogmatic way), in so much as certain activities deemed consciously non-virtuous cannot be applied to her. We will see later how the Catholic church has elevated Mary through all phases of Jungian feminine archetypes.

Sophia

The fourth and final phase of anima development is *Sophia*, named after the Greek word for wisdom. Complete integration has now occurred, which allows females to be seen and related to as particular individuals who possess both positive and negative qualities. The most important aspect of this final level is that, as the personification "Wisdom" suggests, the anima is now developed enough that no single object can fully and permanently contain the images to which it is related. Sophia means wisdom. The name of Wisdom shows up in the Old Testament as a persona, and the consort of God. In Gnostic works, Sophia was the creative force that formed the spirit of man and Sophia was Eve, who came down to offer knowledge to Adam.

When we look at these stages in detail, we notice that within each of these archetypes the church has created evolutionary stages as the body works its way back to a balance of male and female forces.

Eve

Eve – her name means "Mother of All Living, Restorer, Reviver." From Eve all human life descends. She is thus the symbol of fertility and procreation. Throughout the life of the church, women have been equated with Eve and her part in the fall of mankind in the garden. In general, the state of Eve in the male psyche has been one of deep ambivalence. There is an old saying that men hate women as a lame man hates his crutch.

Following are a few quotes from church fathers regarding women and their place in society and religion:

"Rather should the words of the Torah be burned than entrusted to a woman...Whoever teaches his daughter the Torah is like one who teaches her obscenity." ***Rabbi Eliezer***

"Do you not know that you are each an Eve? The sentence of God on this sex of yours lives in this age: the guilt must of necessity live too. You are the Devil's gateway: You are the unsealer of the forbidden tree: You are the first deserter of the divine law: You are she who persuaded him whom the devil was not valiant enough to attack. You destroyed so easily God's image, man. On account of your desertion, even the Son of God had to die." ***St. Tertullian***

"What is the difference whether it is in a wife or a mother, it is still Eve, the temptress that we must beware of in any woman......I fail to see what use woman can be to man, if one excludes the function of bearing children." *St. Augustine of Hippo*

"As regards the individual nature, woman is defective and misbegotten, for the active force in the male seed tends to the production of a perfect likeness in the masculine sex; while the production of woman comes from a defect in the active force or from some material indisposition, or even from some external influence." *St. Thomas Aquinas*

"If they [women] become tired or even die, that does not matter. Let them die in childbirth, that's why they are there." *Martin Luther*

The status of women in the Bible, is disputed. Beginning with Eve herself, there is a dynamic split of position and place, owing to the fact that there are two separate accounts of her creation. The traditional church has seen the role of Eve as mother of Cain and Abel, as well as the person who was deceived into sin by Satan.

Message Bible - Genesis 1:26-28
God spoke: "Let us make human beings in our image, make them reflecting our nature so they can be responsible for the fish in the sea, the birds in the air, the cattle, and, yes, Earth itself, and every animal that moves on the face of Earth."

God created human beings; he created them godlike, reflecting God's nature. He created them male and female. God blessed them: "Prosper! Reproduce! Fill Earth! Take charge!
Be responsible for fish in the sea and birds in the air, for every living thing that moves on the face of Earth."

Genesis 2: 21-22
God put the Man into a deep sleep. As he slept he removed one of his ribs and replaced it with flesh. God then used the rib that he had taken from the Man to make Woman and presented her to the Man. **(23-25)** The Man said, "Finally! Bone of my bone, flesh of my flesh! Name her Woman for she was made from Man." Therefore a man leaves his father and mother and embraces his wife. They become one flesh. The two of them, the Man and his Wife, were naked, but they felt no shame.

In the first account, in Genesis 1:26, woman was made at the same time man was created. In the second account, in Genesis 2: 21, woman was made from man's rib. In the first account, because man and woman were created at the same time, woman was given equal status, but the prevailing ideas of the time would not allow this to stand. It was due to this dual storyline and the fact that women were thought to be inferior to man that the myth of Lilith was born. In this myth, Adam's first wife, Lilith sought to be his equal. The story shows this mindset was thought to be evil.

The Sophia of Jesus and Eugnostos the Blessed

God created all things living, and then he created man. He created a man and a woman and gave them dominion over all things. God named the man Adam, and the woman He named Lilith. Both were formed from the dust of the earth and in both God breathed the breath of life. They became human souls and God endowed them with the power of speech.

Created at the same time, in the same way, there was no master, no leader, and only bickering between them. Lilith said, "I will not be below you, in life or during sex. I want the superior position". But Adam would not relent and insisted God had created him to be the head of the family and in the affairs of earth. Lilith was enraged and would not submit.

Then God communed with Adam in the cool of the evening and as he entered into His presence, Adam appealed to God. As God fellowshipped with them, they reasoned together, Adam, Lilith, and the living God. But Lilith would not listen to God or Adam. Seeing that with two people of equal authority there could be no solution, Lilith became frustrated, angry, and intractable. Finally, enraged and defiant, she pronounced the holy and indescribable name of God. Corrupting the power of the name, she flew into the air, changing form, and disappeared, soaring out of sight.

Adam stood alone, confused, praying. "Lord of the universe," he said, "The woman you gave me has run away." At once, three holy angels were dispatched to bring her back to Adam. The angels overtook Lilith as she passed over the sea, in the area where Moses would later pass through. The angels ordered Lilith to come with them in the name and by the authority of the most high God, but she refused. As her rebellion increased, she changed, becoming more and more ugly and demonic.

God spoke into Lilith's heart, saying, "You have chosen this evil path, and so shall you become evil. You are cursed from now until the end of *days." Lilith spoke to the angels and said, "I have become this, created to cause sickness, to kill children, which I will never have, and to torment men." With these words, she completed her demonic transformation. Her form was that of a succubus.*

Confined to the night, she was destined to roam the earth, seeking newborn babes, stealing their lives, and strangling them in their sleep. She torments men even now, causing lust and evil dreams. Her rebellious and evil spirit forever traps her. Bound in the darkness of her own heart, Lilith became the mistress and lover to legions of demons. And Adam's countenance fell and he mourned, for he had loved Lilith, and he was again alone and lonely.

God said, "It is not good for man to be alone." And the Lord God caused a deep sleep to fall on him, and he slept, and He took from Adam a rib from among his ribs for the woman, and this rib was the origin of the woman. And He built up the flesh in its place, and created the woman. He awakened Adam out of his sleep. On awakening Adam rose on the sixth day, and God brought her to Adam, and he knew her, and said to her, "This is now bone of my bones and flesh of my flesh; she shall be called woman for she was taken from man, and she shall be called my wife; because she was taken from her husband."

Mary Magdalene

Mary Magdalene was the woman delivered from demons by Jesus. She was a woman who was seen as deeply flawed by demonic possession. Being set free by the man, Jesus, she followed him to the end. She was a strong, committed, and determined woman, but she was a woman nonetheless. The apostles challenged Jesus because they believed he would be judged harshly by the masses for being to close to Mary. Recent discoveries have led scholars to believe Magdala, the city that Mary came from and whose name is derived from the place-name, was likely a woman of means. The city was known for its ships and fishing industry. Mary was probably part of the fishing industry and could have owned ships. Mary Magdalene was most likely bankrolling part of he ministry of Jesus.

She was a woman who followed Jesus as he ministered and preached.

Luke 8:1-3: *Afterward, Jesus journeyed from one town and village to another, preaching and proclaiming the good news of the kingdom of God. Accompanying him were the Twelve and some women who had been cured of evil spirits and infirmities, Mary, called Magdalene, from whom seven demons had gone out, Joanna, the wife of Herod's steward Chuza, Susanna, and many others who provided for them out of their resources.*

She was there when Jesus was crucified.

Mark 15:40: *There were also some women looking on from a distance, among whom were Mary Magdalene, and Mary, the mother of James the Less and Joses, and Salome.*

Matthew 27:56: Among them was Mary Magdalene, and Mary, the mother of James and Joseph, and the mother of the sons of Zebedee.

John 19:25: But standing by the cross of Jesus were His mother, and His mother's sister, Mary, the wife of Clopas, and Mary Magdalene.

She continued to believe in Jesus after he was killed.

Mark 15:47: Mary Magdalene and Mary, the mother of Joses, were looking on to see where He was laid.

Matthew 27:61: And Mary Magdalene was there, and the other Mary, sitting opposite the grave.

Matthew 28:1: Now after the Sabbath, as it began to dawn toward the first day of the week, Mary Magdalene and the other Mary came to look at the grave.

Mark 16:1: When the Sabbath was over, Mary Magdalene, and Mary, the mother of James, and Salome, bought spices, so that they might come and anoint Him.

She was the first to realize and announce the resurrection of Jesus.

John 20:1: Now, on the first day of the week, Mary Magdalene came early to the tomb, while it was still dark, and saw the stone already taken away from the tomb.

Mark 16:9: *Now after He had risen early on the first day of the week, He first appeared to Mary Magdalene, from whom He had cast out seven demons.*

John 20:18: *Mary Magdalene came, announcing to the disciples, "I have seen the Lord," and that He had said these things to her.*

Luke 24: *But at daybreak on the first day of the week [the women] took the spices they had prepared and went to the tomb. They found the stone rolled away from the tomb; but when they entered, they did not find the body of the Lord Jesus. While they were puzzling over this, behold, two men in dazzling garments appeared to them. They were terrified and bowed their faces to the ground. They said to them, "Why do you seek the living one among the dead?*

He is not here, but he has been raised. Remember what he said to you while he was still in Galilee, that the Son of Man must be handed over to sinners and be crucified, and rise on the third day." And they remembered his words.

Then they returned from the tomb and announced all these things to the eleven and to all the others.

The women were Mary Magdalene, Joanna, and Mary, the mother of James; the others who accompanied them also told this to the apostles, but their story seemed like nonsense and they did not believe them.

Most Gnostic Christians held to the idea of the duality of sexes playing out in multiple layers. The feminine force of Sophia becomes the feminine force of the Holy Spirit and is made the bride of God. The gender duality continues when the feminine force of the Holy Spirit inhabits the perfect man, Jesus, making him the Messiah. The gender context is ripe for the story to be continued in the persons of Jesus and Mary Magdalene, physically shadowing the spiritual relationship of the Holy Spirit and the Supreme God, as well as Jesus and the Holy Spirit.

The concept of a married Jesus is revealed in several verses of The Gospel of Philip, such as verse 118.

"There is the Son of Man and there is the son of the son of Man. The Lord is the Son of Man, and his son creates through him. God gave the Son of Man the power to create; he also gave him the ability to have children."

If one were to examine the writings of Solomon, the play on words between the masculine and feminine, and the spiritual aspects can be seen clearly. The Gnostics simply expanded on the theme.

Song of Solomon 1 (King James Version)
1 The song of songs, which is Solomon's.
2 Let him kiss me with the kisses of his mouth: for thy love is better than wine.

3 Because of the savour of thy good ointments thy name is as ointment poured forth, therefore do the virgins love thee.
4 Draw me, we will run after thee: the king hath brought me into his chambers: we will be glad and rejoice in thee, we will remember thy love more than wine.

Song of Solomon 2

16 My beloved is mine, and I am his: he feedeth among the lilies.
17 Until the day break, and the shadows flee away, turn, my beloved, and be thou like a roe or a young hart upon the mountains of Bether.

Song of Solomon 3

1 By night on my bed I sought him whom my soul loveth: I sought him, but I found him not.
2 I will rise now, and go about the city in the streets, and in the broad ways I will seek him whom my soul loveth: I sought him, but I found him not...

Song of Solomon 5

1 I am come into my garden, my sister, my spouse: I have gathered my myrrh with my spice; I have eaten my honeycomb with my honey; I have drunk my wine with my milk: eat, O friends; drink, yea, drink abundantly, O beloved.
2 I sleep, but my heart waketh: it is the voice of my beloved that knocketh, saying, Open to me, my sister, my love, my dove, my undefiled: for my head is filled with dew, and my locks with the drops of the night.

3 I have put off my coat; how shall I put it on? I have washed my feet; how shall I defile them?

4 My beloved put in his hand by the hole of the door, and my bowels were moved for him.

5 I rose up to open to my beloved; and my hands dropped with myrrh, and my fingers with sweet smelling myrrh, upon the handles of the lock.

Song of Solomon 7

1 How beautiful are thy feet with shoes, O prince's daughter! the joints of thy thighs are like jewels, the work of the hands of a cunning workman.

2 Thy navel is like a round goblet, which wanteth not liquor: thy belly is like an heap of wheat set about with lilies.

3 Thy two breasts are like two young roes that are twins.

Due to the inherent dualism of Gnosticism, sex was a symbol, and at times, a portal to a mystical experience. This is one reason the Aeons were said to be created in pairs on male and female. It is also why the texts of The Sophia of Jesus Christ and Eugnostos the Blessed refers to the Aeon and to Jesus as "androgynous" which indicates the existence of both make and female energies. Within the contexts we find in Jesus both male and female powers. Gnosticism seeks a balance of energies, both in the spiritual realm and the physical world. For this reason the Aeons were made in pairs.

The balance or compliment to Jesus is Sophia. Even the supreme and indescribable God had his counterpart in Barbelo. Barbelo is often depicted as a supreme female principle, the single passive

The Sophia of Jesus and Eugnostos the Blessed

antecedent of creation in its infinite forms. She is called the 'Mother-Father', again hinting at androgyny. She is called 'First Human Being', and 'Eternal Aeon'. So prominent was her place amongst some Gnostics that some schools were designated as Barbeliotae, or Barbelognostics.

Keeping in mind that Gnosticism is an amalgam of Plato's cosmology and Christian theology, it is interesting to note Plato's "Split Apart Theory." Plato's theory was that each human being is part of one soul, having both male and female parts, in which they only have half. The idea is that the soul was "split-apart" and separated from each other at the time the soul left heavenly realm. The two halves have been forever searching for one another in order to join together and regain their sense of original created wholeness. Thus, we, in our wholeness, exhibit the same androgyny as the Aeons when we are in our completed state with our "split apart." For this and other reasons, many Gnostic schools believed sex was a portal to a mystical experience.

The idea of completeness in sex and the need for a gender balance in religion was a well-established concept in Gnosticism and their influence on the sects of Christianity that became mainline should not be overlooked. Many religions are replete with sexual allegories, as is Gnosticism. Proceeding from the point of view that people, like aeons, need a complement and balance of male and female energies in Gnostic literature and the likelihood of marriage among the population of Jewish men, controversy arose as to whether Jesus could have married, or should have been married to achieve his "fullness". The flames of argument roared into inferno proportions when the translation of the books of Philip and Mary Magdalene were published.

"And the companion (Consort) was Mary of Magdala (Mary Magdalene). The Lord loved Mary more than all the other disciples and he kissed her often on her mouth (the text is missing here and the word "mouth" is assumed). The others saw his love for Mary and asked him: "Why do you love her more than all of us?" The Savior replied, "Why do I not love you in the same way I love her?"
  The Gospel of Philip

Peter said to Mary; "Sister we know that the Savior loved you more than all other women. Tell us the words of the Savior that you remember and know, but we have not heard and do not know. Mary answered him and said; "I will tell you what He hid from you."
  The Gospel of Mary Magdalene

Mary was a sinful, damaged, redeemed, powerful person. It is the myth woven into the story of Mary Magdalene that empowers her to us. To many, she is the captive. Possessed, enslaved, caught in the midst of crime and tragedy, but at once redeemed, set free, and loved by God himself. (Mary was connected to the story of a prostitute, but this is not the case.) She is hope and triumph. She represents the power of truth and love to change the life of the lowest and most powerless of us. She is you and me in search of God.

Mary, The Mother of Jesus

The evolution of the status of Mary, the mother of Jesus, is the attempt by the collective psyche of the church to find the correct place for the feminine energies of God. However, since the church leaders have not reconciled the balance of masculine and feminine parts of God, Mary was chosen as a surrogate to be endowed with some of these qualities.

Rising to another level of the Sacred Feminine, *Ruak* becomes the female part of the Godhead that impregnated Mary to produce Jesus. The same spirit empowered Jesus by coming down in the visage of a dove. Mary was visited and carried this spirit within her womb. It is natural that she would come to be equated with the same mothering, nurturing, Sacred Feminine.

The Catholic Church was diminishing the status of women at the same time as they struggled to make sense of their own female redeemer. They began to elevate Mother Mary by announcing the doctrine of the Immaculate Conception, so errors in logic were exposed. If Mother Mary was conceived without sin in order to carry Jesus, who was conceived without sin, one must ask why wasn't it necessary for the mother of Mary to also be conceived without sin. This logic continues backward ad infinitum until Eve herself and all female offspring must be sinless. Of course, the church flatly refuses this line of reasoning, saying only that certain things must be taken on faith. This is the same tactic taken regarding the "Ever-Virginity" of Mother Mary, even in the face of scriptures proclaiming that the mother, sister, and brothers of Jesus had come to have audience with him.

It was the Greek Orthodox Church that already had the answer to this dilemma. Original sin is not in their doctrine. They state only that humans are born with a pre-disposition toward sinning. This makes the problem of sinless birth from the beginning, null.

Even though the theological events of doctrine concerning Mother Mary occurred over time, they serve as an undeniable pattern of the Catholic Church as it endeavored to "purify" women and rid them of sexuality. It is within Mary that we find the complete evolution of the Sacred Feminine, but with sexuality systematically muted and removed.

Beginning as a teenage girl, dismissed by society as a lowly female, she has, over time, been elevated to a position wherein the Catholic Church has placed her alongside, although not quite equal to, the savior himself. Some of the positions of the Catholic Church regarding Mary were not officially accepted until the mid to late nineteenth century.

The Sophia of Jesus and Eugnostos the Blessed

In the writings of the early church fathers (Justin Martyr 165 A.D. and Irenaeus 202 A.D.), Mother Mary was seldom mentioned and only to contrast Mary's obedience with Eve's disobedience.

The doctrine of Mary as Theotokos (God-bearer) probably originated in Alexandria and was first introduced by Origen. It became common in the fourth century and accepted at the Council of Ephesus in 431 A.D.

Since the accepted Christian church continued to slip farther and farther toward the belief that sex was evil, the doctrine of the "Ever-Virginity" of Mary was established. This was the belief that Mary conceived as a virgin, but also remained a virgin even after giving birth to Jesus and thereafter, for the rest of her life. The Catholic Church rejects the idea that Mary had other children, although the Bible speaks of the brothers and sisters of Jesus. The doctrine of "virginity" was established around 359 A.D.

The doctrine of the bodily Assumption of Mary was formally developed by St. Gregory of Tours around 594 A.D. This doctrine stated that Mary, the mother of Jesus, was taken up into heaven to be seated at the side of Jesus. The idea has been present in apocryphal texts since the late fourth century. The Feast of the Assumption became widespread in the sixth century, and sermons on that occasion tended to emphasize Mary's power in heaven.

Of all the doctrines regarding Mary, the doctrine of the Immaculate Conception widened the divide between the Catholic churches and other Christian churches. This doctrine took the position that Mother Mary was born without the stain of original sin. Both Catholics and Orthodox Christians accept this doctrine, but only the Roman Catholic Church has named it "The Immaculate Conception" and articulated it as doctrine.

Eastern Orthodox Christians reject the western doctrine of original sin, preferring instead to speak of a tendency towards sin. They believe Mary was born without sin, but so was everyone else. Mary simply never gave in to sin.

As we see in the following statement, the doctrine was not formally accepted until 1854 A.D. "The Most Blessed Virgin Mary was, from the first moment of her conception, by a singular grace and privilege of almighty God and by virtue of the merits of Jesus Christ, Savior of the human race, preserved immune from all stain of original sin."
Pope Pius IX, Ineffabilis Deus (1854)

We will examine the four Marian dogmas, among a large number of other teachings about Mary, and how they mirror the evolution of the Scared Feminine.

Perpetual Virginity – Established in the Third Century – Proclaims that Mary was a virgin before, during, and after the birth of Jesus.

Mother of God – First Council of Ephesus in 431 A.D. - Mary is truly the mother of God, because of her unity with Christ, the Son of God.

Immaculate Conception – Pope Pius IX (1854) Mary, at her conception, was preserved immaculate from the original sin.

Assumption into Heaven – Pope Pius XII (1950) - Mary, having completed the course of her earthly life, was assumed body and soul into heavenly glory.

'Perpetual Virginity of Mary', means that Mary was a virgin before, during and after giving birth.

Mary was a teenage unwed mother in a world where such things brought shame and death by stoning. Beginning in the general status as Eve, stressing only her lowly station as a younger woman married to an older man for the purpose of procreation and service, she is raised by the doctrine of "Ever-Virginity" to one that is a step above the norm, being without sin when it comes to her primary purpose of procreation.

This oldest Marian dogma from the Roman Catholic, Eastern Orthodox, and Oriental Orthodox Churches affirms in their doctrine that the virginity of Mary, mother of Jesus is "real and perpetual even in the act of giving birth to the Son of God made

Man." According to this doctrine, Jesus was her only biological son, whose incarnation and nativity are miraculous.

In the year 107 A.D. Ignatius of Antioch described the virginity of Mary as "hidden from the prince of this world ... loudly proclaimed, but wrought in the silence of God." The Gospel of James, a text written around 120-150 A.D., was concerned with the character and purity of Mary. The text claims that Joseph had children from a marriage previous to Mary. However, the text does not explicitly assert the doctrine of perpetual virginity. The earliest such surviving reference is Origen's *Commentary on Matthew*, where he cites the *Protoevangelium* in support.

By the fourth century, the doctrine was generally accepted. Athanasius described Mary as "Ever-Virgin".

In Thomas Aquinas' teaching, (*Summa Theologiae* III.28.2), Mary gave birth painlessly in miraculous fashion without opening of the womb and without injury to the hymen. *"From the first formulations of her faith, the Church has confessed that Jesus was conceived solely by the power of the Holy Spirit in the womb of the Virgin Mary, affirming also the corporeal aspect of this event: Jesus was conceived "by the Holy Spirit without human seed."*

Her corporal integrity was not affected by giving birth. The Church does not teach how this occurred physically, but insists that virginity during child birth is different from virginity of conception. *Pope Pius XII*

Mystici Corporis: "Within her virginal womb she brought into life Christ our Lord in a marvelous birth." This indicated the miraculous nature of the Virgin birth. In fact, this was the first act that would remove the stain of sex from Mary, making her a virgin forever. She is now a woman removed from the natural cause and effect of her sexuality.

Mary is truly the *Mother of God.*
Even though Mary was clear of adultery, as Joseph first thought when she announced her pregnancy, and the sin of coitus was removed from her by declaring her a perpetual virgin, when it comes to procreation, she remains a woman in service to men, being different from other women, but not reverenced. In this proclamation, the church elevates Mary to the heights of womanhood, announcing that she is "Theotokos", Mother-of-God, where she begins to be honored.

After the Church fathers found common ground on Mary's virginity before, during, and after giving birth, this was the first specifically Marian doctrine to be formally defined by the Church. The definition *Mother of God* (in Greek: Theotokos) was formally affirmed at the held at Third Ecumenical Council in Ephesus in 431 A.D. The competing view, advocated by the Patriarch of Constantinople, Nestorius of Constantinople, was that Mary should be called *Christotokos*, meaning, "Birth-giver of Christ," to restrict her role to the mother of Christ's humanity only and not his divine nature.

The holy virgin gave birth in the flesh to God united with the flesh according to hypostasis, and for that reason, we call her *Theotokos*... If anyone does not confess that Emmanuel is, in truth, God, and, therefore, that the holy virgin is *Theotokos* (for she bore, in a fleshly manner, the Word from God become flesh), let him be anathema (banned, exiled, excommunicated)." *(Cyril's third letter to Nestorius)*

Immaculate Conception of Mary
Mary was conceived without original sin.
For Mary to be so different from other women, there must have been a divine intervention from the beginning. The answer was a miracle that kept Mary from the sin of being fully human, for to be fully human, according to the church, one would be born as a sinful creature. This is the first doctrine to hint that the most righteous woman could be as sinless as the most righteous man, Jesus. Both were conceived without sin.

According to the Roman Catholic Church, Immaculate Conception is the conception of a child without any stain of original sin in her mother's womb: the dogma states that, from the first moment of her existence, she (Mary) was preserved by God from the sin that afflicts mankind, and that she was instead filled with Divine Grace.

It is further believed that she lived a life completely free from sin. Her immaculate conception in the womb of her mother, by normal coitus (Christian tradition identifies her parents as Joachim and Anne), should not be confused with the doctrine of the virginal conception of her son, Jesus.

The feast of the Immaculate Conception, celebrated on December 8, was established in 1476 by Pope Sixtus IV. Pope Pius IX, in his constitution *Ineffabilis Deus*, on December 8, 1854, solemnly defined the Immaculate Conception as a dogma, a truth, not merely an implied condition, by the deposit of faith, and discerned by the Church under the infallible guidance of the Holy Spirit. However, the dogma is specifically and explicitly contained as an object of supernatural faith in the Public Revelation of the Deposit of Faith.

Mary is Mother of all Christians – 1579 A.D.
Obedience to God, perfect faith, and the church's position, which removed Mary from the sin that besets all who are "born of woman" has positioned Mary as the perfect mother. God has been born from her sinless body. She has raised and mothered God himself. In doing so, she has given birth to the church. Now she is given the status of the greatest mother in the world and is crowned as "Mother of all Christians." Still, Mary is identified only as a woman and a mother, but she is now the zenith and apex of these things.

The Catholic Church teaches that the Virgin Mary is mother of the Church and of all its members, namely all Christians. The Catechism of the Catholic Church states:

"The Virgin Mary . . . is acknowledged and honoured as being truly the Mother of God and of the redeemer.... She is 'clearly the mother of the members of Christ' . . . since she has by her charity joined in bringing about the birth of believers in the Church, who are members of its head." "Mary, Mother of Christ, Mother of the Church."

Mary is seen as mother of all Christians because Christians are said in scripture to become spiritually part of the body of Christ and Mary bore Christ in her body. Christians are adopted by Jesus as his "brothers". They therefore share with Him the Fatherhood of God and also the motherhood of Mary. To back up this stance, in the Book of John, Jesus, gives the Apostle John to Mary as her son, and gives Mary to John as his mother as he is about to die. John here, as the sole remaining Apostle remaining steadfast with Jesus, is taken to represent all loyal followers of Jesus from that time on.

Pope John Paul II , in his work, "Totus Tuus" was inspired by the writings of Saint Louis de Montfort on total consecration to the Virgin Mary, which he quoted:.

"Now, since Mary is of all creatures the one most conformed to Jesus Christ, it follows that among all devotions that which most consecrates and conforms a soul to our Lord is devotion to Mary, his Holy Mother, and

that the more a soul is consecrated to her the more will it be consecrated to Jesus Christ."

Assumption of Mary
Mary was assumed into heaven with body and soul.
As time went on, the church removed women from positions of authority and spiritual leadership. The assumption of Mary in 1950 places a woman at the throne of God, beside her son, Jesus. She has surpassed being a mother and is now bodily in heaven, placing her in the company of only three others: Jesus, Elijah, and Enoch, who were also taken up to heaven in physical form.

Mary, the ever virgin, mother of God was free of original sin. The Immaculate Conception is one basis for the 1950 dogma. Another was the century old Church-wide veneration of the Virgin Mary as being assumed into heaven, which Pope Pius XII referred to in *Deiparae Virginis Mariae*. Although the assumption of Mary was only recently defined as dogma, accounts of the bodily assumption of Mary into heaven have circulated, at least, since the 5th century. The Catholic Church itself interprets chapter 12 of the Book of Revelation as referring to it. The story appears in "The Passing of the Virgin Mary", a late 5th century work ascribed to Melito of Sardis and tells the story of the apostles being transported by white clouds to the death-bed of Mary, each from the town where he was preaching at the hour.

Theological debate about the Assumption continued until 1950 when, in the Apostolic Constitution, Munificentissimus Deus, it was defined as definitive doctrine by Pope Pius XII.

"We pronounce, declare, and define it to be a divinely revealed dogma: that the Immaculate Mother of God, the ever Virgin Mary, having completed the course of her earthly life, was assumed body and soul into heavenly glory."

Since the 1870 solemn declaration of Papal Infallibility by the Vatican I, this declaration by Pope Pius XII has been the only use of Papal Infallibility. While Pope Pius XII deliberately left open the question of whether Mary died before her Assumption, the more common teaching of the early Fathers is that she did. "

After the proclamation of the assumption of Mary, Carl Jung wrote:

"The promulgation of the new dogma of the Assumption of the Virgin Mary could, in itself, have been sufficient reason for examining the psychological background. It is interesting to note that, among the many articles published in the Catholic and Protestant press on the declaration of the dogma, there was not one, so far as I could see, which laid anything like proper emphasis on what was undoubtedly the most powerful motive: namely the popular movement and the psychological need behind it."

Essentially, the writers of the articles were satisfied with learned considerations, dogmatic and historical, which have no bearing on the living religious process. But anyone who has followed with attention the visions of Mary which have been increasing in number over the last few decades, and has taken their psychological significance into account, might have known what was brewing.

The fact, especially, that it was largely children who had the visions might have given pause for thought, for in such cases, the collective unconscious is always at work ...One could have known for a long time that there was a deep longing in the masses for an intercessor and mediatrix who would at last take her place alongside the Holy Trinity and be received as the 'Queen of heaven and Bride at the heavenly court.' For more than a thousand years it has been taken for granted that the Mother of God dwelt there.

I consider it to be the most important religious event since the Reformation. It is a petra scandali for the unpscholgical mind: how can such an unfounded assertion as the bodily reception of the Virgin into heaven be put forward as worthy of belief? But the method which the Pope uses in order to demonstrate the truth of the dogma makes sense to the psychological mind, because it bases itself firstly on the necessary prefigurations, and secondly on a tradition of religious assertions reaching back for more than a thousand years.

What outrages the Protestant standpoint in particular is the boundless approximation of the Deipara to the Godhead and, in consequence, the endangered supremacy of Christ, from which Protestantism will not budge. In sticking to this point it has obviously failed to consider that its hymnology is full of references to the 'heavenly bridegroom,' who is now suddenly supposed not to have a bride with equal rights. Or has, perchance, the 'bridegroom,' in true psychologistic manner, been understood as a mere metaphor?

The dogmatizing of the Assumption does not, however, according to the dogmatic view, mean that Mary has attained the status of goddess, although, as mistress of heaven and a mediator, she is functionally on a par with Christ, the King and mediator. At any rate her position satisfies a renewed hope for the fulfillment of that yearning for peace which stirs deep down in the soul, and for a resolution of the threatening tension between opposites. Everyone shares this tension and everyone experiences it in his individual form of unrest. The more unrest he has, the less he sees any possibility of getting rid of it by rational means. It is no wonder, therefore, that the hope, indeed, the expectation of divine intervention arises in the collective unconscious and, at the same time, in the masses. The papal declaration has given comforting expression to that yearning. "How could Protestantism so completely miss the point?"
("The Answer to Job" by Carl Jung)

Mary as Mediatrix

Although this position does not make her equal to God or his son, it does acknowledge that there is now a feminine influence and energy in Heaven. With compassion and caring, the church has her whispering her counsel and wisdom into the ear of her son, the Savior.

In Catholic teachings, Jesus Christ is the only mediator between God and man, although priests may intercede. He alone reconciled, through his death on the cross, creator and creation. But this does not exclude a secondary mediating role for Mary. The teaching that Mary intercedes for all believers, especially those who request her intercession through prayer, has been held in the Church since early times, for example by Ephraim, the Syrian "after the mediator, a mediatrix for the whole world." Intercession is something that may be done by all the heavenly saints, but Mary is seen as having the greatest intercessory power. The earliest surviving recorded prayer to Mary is the *Subtuum Praesidium*, written in Greek around 250 A.D.

Mary has increasingly been seen as a principal dispenser of God's graces and an advocate for the people of God. She is mentioned as such in several official Church documents. Pope Pius IX used the title in the *Ineffabilis Deus Supremi Apostolatus.* In the first of his so called *Rosary Encyclicals*, (1883), Pope Leo XIII calls Our Lady, *The guardian of our peace and the dispensatrix of heavenly graces.* In his 1954 Encyclical, *Ad Caeli Reginam,* Pope Pius XII calls Mary the Mediatrix of peace.

Co-Redemptrix
This position is not doctrine, but is held as a position by many in the church. The idea was once again submitted for consideration as dogma in the late 1990's. The idea submitted by the church that Mary is Co-Redemptrix places her above all men, save one. She is

now raised above those others with bodily form in heaven, except Jesus himself. At this point, Mary has been promoted.

Co-Redemptrix refers to the participation of Mary in the salvation process. Already, Irenaeus, the Church Father (Died 200 A.D.), referred to Mary as "causa salutis" [cause of our salvation], acknowledging her authority formally. It is teaching, which has been considered since the 15th century but never declared a dogma. The Roman Catholic view of Co-Redemptrix does not imply that Mary participates as equal part in the redemption of the human race, since Christ is the only redeemer. Mary herself needed redemption and was redeemed by Jesus Christ her son. Being redeemed by Christ, implies that she cannot be his equal in the redemption process. (It seems that in this part of the doctrine Mary was born without original sin, but must have later sinned in some way in order to need redemption.)

Co-redemptrix refers to an indirect or unequal but important participation by Mary in the redemption process. She gave free consent to give life to the redeemer, to share his life, to suffer with him under the cross and to sacrifice him for the sake of the redemption of mankind. Co-redemption is not something new.

Queen of Heaven
The doctrine that the Virgin Mary has been crowned Queen of Heaven, "the Mother of the King of the universe," and the "Virgin

The Sophia of Jesus and Eugnostos the Blessed

Mother who brought forth the King of the whole world" goes back to St. Gregory Nazianzen. The Catholic Church often sees Mary as queen in heaven, bearing a crown of twelve stars in the Book of Revelation.

The evolution of the status of Mary, the Mother of Jesus has taken eighteen-hundred years to become what it is today. The king of glory now has a queen and the balance is restored in the mind of the church. But this balance is a false one and does not fulfill the reunification of the vital male and female energies in the one and only God. With Mary, there is still duality, and duality is not an acceptable answer to the unity found within one God and spirit.

Wisdom – Sophia

Sophia has a double meaning within Christian theology owing to the split within the early church between orthodoxy and Gnosticism. Wisdom within orthodox (mainstream) Christianity is presented as a spirit entity and consort of God. The book of Proverbs is a well known book of the Bible. The book of Wisdom is found in the Bibles of the Catholic Church and Orthodox Church. The verses here reflect the reverence of wisdom within the church, but they did not view her as a entity or the consort of God, even though the texts state that she is. Wisdom became directly connected with the Logos of the New Testament. Later, we will discuss the place of Sophia within lesser known sects such as the Gnostic Church.

Proverbs 8

22) The Lord created me first of all, the first of his works, long ago.
23) I was made in the very beginning, at the first, before the world began.
24) I was born before the oceans, when there were no springs of water.
25) I was born before the mountains, before the hills were set in place,
26) before God made the earth and its fields or even the first handful of soil.
27) I was there when he set the sky in place, when he stretched the horizon across the ocean,
28) when he placed the clouds in the sky, when he opened the springs of the ocean
29) and ordered the waters of the sea to rise no further than he said. I was there when he laid the earth's foundations.
30) I was beside him like an architect. I was his daily source of joy, always happy in his presence,
31) happy with the world and pleased with the human race.
32) Now, young people, listen to me. Do as I say, and you will be happy.
33) Listen to what you are taught. Be wise; do not neglect it.
34) Those who listen to me will be happy, those who stay at my door every day, waiting at the entrance to my home.
35) Those who find me find life, and the Lord will be pleased with them.

36) Those who do not find me hurt themselves; anyone who hates me loves death.

The Book of Wisdom 7
(Apocrypha and Orthodox Bible)

21) I learned things that were well known and things that had never been known before,
22) because Wisdom, who gave shape to everything that exists, was my teacher.

The Nature of Wisdom

23) The spirit of Wisdom is intelligent and holy. It is of one nature, but reveals itself in many ways. It is not made of any material substance, and it moves about freely. It is clear, clean, and confident; it cannot be harmed. It loves what is good. It is sharp and unconquerable, kind, and a friend of humanity. It is dependable and sure, and has no worries. It has power over everything, and sees everything. It penetrates every spirit that is intelligent and pure, no matter how delicate its substance may be.
24) Wisdom moves more easily than motion itself; she is so pure that she penetrates everything.
25) She is a breath of God's power a pure and radiant stream of glory from the Almighty. Nothing that is defiled can ever steal its way into Wisdom.
26) She is a reflection of eternal light, a perfect mirror of God's activity and goodness.

27) Even though Wisdom acts alone, she can do anything. She makes everything new, although she herself never changes. From generation to generation she enters the souls of holy people, and makes them God's friends and prophets.

28) There is nothing that God loves more than people who are at home with Wisdom.

29) Wisdom is more beautiful than the sun and all the constellations. She is better than light itself,

30) because night always follows day, but evil never overcomes Wisdom.

Wisdom 8

1) Her great power reaches into every part of the world, and she sets everything in useful order.

Solomon's Love for Wisdom

2) Wisdom has been my love. I courted her when I was young and wanted to make her my bride. I fell in love with her beauty.

3) She glorifies her noble origin by living with God, the Lord of all, who loves her.

4) She is familiar with God's mysteries and helps determine his course of action.

5) Is it good to have riches in this life? Nothing can make you richer than Wisdom, who makes everything function.

6) Is knowledge a useful thing to have? Nothing is better than Wisdom, who has given shape to everything that exists.

7) Do you love justice? All the virtues are the result of Wisdom's work: justice and courage, self-control and understanding. Life can offer us nothing more valuable than these.

8) Do you want to have wide experience? Wisdom knows the lessons of history and can anticipate the future. She knows how to interpret what people say and how to solve problems. She knows the miracles that God will perform, and how the movements of history will develop.

Wisdom 9

Solomon Prays for Wisdom

1) God of my ancestors, merciful Lord, by your word you created everything.

2) By your Wisdom you made us humans to rule all creation,

3) to govern the world with holiness and righteousness, to administer justice with integrity.

4) Give me the Wisdom that sits beside your throne; give me a place among your children.

5) I am your slave, as was my mother before me. I am only human. I am not strong, and my life will be short. I have little understanding of the Law or of how to apply it.

6) Even if someone is perfect, he will be thought of as nothing without the Wisdom that comes from you.

7) You chose me over everyone else to be the king of your own people, to judge your sons and daughters.

8) You told me to build a temple on your sacred mountain, an altar in Jerusalem, the city you chose as your home. It is a copy of that temple in heaven, which you prepared at the beginning.

9) Wisdom is with you and knows your actions; she was present when you made the world. She knows what pleases you, what is right and in accordance with your commands.

10) Send her from the holy heavens, down from your glorious throne, so that she may work at my side, and I may learn what pleases you.

11) She knows and understands everything, and will guide me intelligently in what I do. Her glory will protect me.

12) Then I will judge your people fairly, and be worthy of my father's throne. My actions will be acceptable.

13) Who can ever learn the will of God?

14) Human reason is not adequate for the task, and our philosophies tend to mislead us,

15) because our mortal bodies weigh our souls down. The body is a temporary structure made of earth, a burden to the active mind.

16) All we can do is make guesses about things on earth; we must struggle to learn about things that are close to us. Who, then, can ever hope to understand heavenly things?

17) No one has ever learned your will, unless you first gave him Wisdom, and sent your holy spirit down to him.

18) In this way, people on earth have been set on the right path, have learned what pleases you, and have been kept safe by Wisdom.

Proverbs 1
Wisdom Calls

20) Listen! Wisdom is calling out in the streets and marketplaces,
21) calling loudly at the city gates and wherever people come together:
22) Foolish people! How long do you want to be foolish? How long will you enjoy making fun of knowledge? Will you never learn?
23) Listen when I reprimand you; I will give you good advice and share my knowledge with you.
24) I have been calling you, inviting you to come, but you would not listen. You paid no attention to me.
25) You have ignored all my advice and have not been willing to let me correct you.
26) So when you get into trouble, I will laugh at you. I will make fun of you when terror strikes
27) when it comes on you like a storm, bringing fierce winds of trouble, and you are in pain and misery.
28) Then you will call for wisdom, but I will not answer. You may look for me everywhere, but you will not find me.
29) You have never had any use for knowledge and have always refused to obey the Lord.
30) You have never wanted my advice or paid any attention when I corrected you.

31) So then, you will get what you deserve, and your own actions will make you sick.

32) Inexperienced people die because they reject wisdom. Stupid people are destroyed by their own lack of concern.

33) But whoever listens to me will have security. He will be safe, with no reason to be afraid.

Sophia, in Gnostic theology, is a creative, spiritual person. In one Gnostic creation story, the Archons (lesser angels) created Adam, but could not bring him to life. In other stories, Adam was formed as a type of worm, unable to attain personhood. Thus, man began as an incomplete creation. In this myth, the Archons were afraid that if Adam were fully formed, he might be more powerful than the Archons themselves. When they saw Adam was incapable of attaining the human state, their fears were put to rest, thus, they called that day the "Day of Rest."

Sophia saw Adam's horrid state and had compassion. Sophia descended to help bring Adam out of his hopeless condition. It is this story that set the stage for the emergence of the Sacred Feminine force in Gnosticism that is not seen in orthodox Christianity. Sophia brought within herself the light and power of the Supreme God. Metaphorically, within the spiritual womb of Sophia was carried the life force of the Supreme God for Adam's salvation as seen in the Gnostic text, "*The Apocryphon of John.*"

The Sophia of Jesus and Eugnostos the Blessed

As the emerging orthodox church became more and more oppressive to women, later even labeling them "occasions of sin," the Gnostics countered by raising women to equal status with men, saying that Sophia was, in a sense, the handmaiden or wife of the Supreme God, making the soul of Adam her spiritual offspring.

Sophia represents the highest and purest attributes of the feminine energies. Sophia is intelligent, independent, powerful, creative, caring, nurturing, and a goddess in her own right. She is the consort of God.

Who is She?

Sophia (fem. Gk. for "wisdom") is a complex biblical figure described variously as a divine attribute, a distinct hypostasis of God, a goddess-like co-partner with God, and sometimes even as synonymous with God. She arises in the later texts of the Jewish tradition, first simply as wisdom with a capital "W," and then, in the Book of Proverbs, personified in a female form. The writings of early Christianity frequently draw on Sophia as a metaphor for Christ. The texts that include references to Sophia have only been canonized in Roman Catholicism and Eastern Orthodoxy, but many contemporary feminists have turned to her as a general model for feminist spirituality.

Her personality is riddled with contradictions. She is at once creator and created; teacher and that which is to be taught; divine presence and elusive knowledge; tempting harlot and faithful wife; sister, lover, and mother; both human and divine. Her very existence thus deconstructs all traditional binary relationships, as if she were the creation of Hélène Cixous, Luce Irigaray or some other modern feminist theorist. Frequently Sophia defies the feminine norm established by society. As Virginia Mollenkott writes in The Divine Feminine, Sophia "is a woman but no lady." (Mollenkott 98). We see her crying aloud at street corners, raising her voice in the public squares, offering her saving counsel to anybody who will listen to her. Wisdom's behavior runs directly counter to the socialization of a proper lady, who is taught to be rarely seen and even more rarely heard in the sphere of public activity. (Mollenkott 98)

Her Origins

Just as Sophia defies definition, her origins seem impossible to trace. Scholars have suggested Semitic sources (the goddess of love and fertility, Ishtar), Egyptian sources (Maat, the goddess of conception), and Hellenistic sources (the goddesses Demeter, Persephone, Hecate, and Isis), and yet they have found no source for Sophia within the Hebrew tradition. Thus, it is still unclear whether she was borrowed from a nearby civilization or invented by the Hebrew writings. Scholars have dated Sophia's textual sources at least 500 years after most of the Hebrew tradition was developed. Sophia can be found in The Book of Proverbs, Wisdom of Solomon, Ecclesiasticus (Ben Sirach), and in the Christian Gospels and epistles.

Her Development

According to the authors of Wisdom's Feast, only God, Job, Moses and David are treated in greater depth in the Hebrew Scriptures than Sophia. (Cady et. al. 15). She grows in power throughout these texts, until, as Christian feminist Joan Chamberlain Engelsman suggests, Sophia comes to rival God's power, promising salvation for those who choose to follow her.

However, the extent of Sophia's divinity in this period has been widely debated. Both Engelsman and Rosemary Radford Ruether insist that the strictly monotheistic texts of Roman-era Judaism never portray Sophia as an autonomous female divine figure. Others have argued that some passages actually describe Sophia as a co-partner with God.

Early Christians seeking to understand Jesus as savior within the context of their Jewish origins searched the Hebrew Scriptures for related figures. Jesus did not completely match the traditional Jewish conception of the messiah who was to be a human king who would establish a new reign of justice and peace in Israel. Jesus actually seemed to have much more in common with Sophia who was part divine and part human, sent by God to change society. And, as the authors of Wisdom's Feast argue, both Christ and Sophia ultimately failed to completely transform society: Sophia's cries to humanity were in vain and Jesus was crucified. Thus, early

Christians adopted Sophia as a model for their portrayals of Christ while continuing to refer to him as the messiah.

Paul makes the following associations between Christ and Sophia: Christ is the Wisdom of God; like Sophia, he is a creator, first born of all creation, the radiance of God's glory and the image of the invisible God. Luke describes Jesus as Sophia's son who communicates her wisdom to humanity. In Matthew's writings, Jesus is explicitly described as personified Wisdom. Perhaps John's Gospel draws the strongest connection between the two figures, relating the story of Sophia as the pre-history of Jesus.

The Disappearance of Sophia

Eventually Sophia was completely fused with Christ. Wisdom became Logos, and explicit associations between Sophia and Jesus disappeared from Christianity. Many Christian feminists describe her disappearance in the psychological language of repression. In her essay, "Wisdom Was Made Flesh," Elizabeth Johnson argues that the feminine Wisdom was replaced by the masculine Logos "as it became unseemly, given the developing patriarchal tendencies in the church, to interpret the male Jesus with a female symbol of God" (Johnson 105). The authors of Wisdom's Feast offer a very different theory. They suggest that in order to recognize Jesus as equal to God the Father, all explicit associations between Jesus and the weaker Sophia had to be abandoned.

The Sophia of Jesus and Eugnostos the Blessed

Wisdom's Feast also traces Sophia's disappearance to the tensions at this time between the Gnostics and the mainstream Christians. The Gnostics tended to downplay Jesus' humanity, and many rejected the notion that he was human. They adopted the association between Jesus and Sophia in order to de-emphasize Christ's bodily pain and suffering and focus more on the wisdom he imparted. Mainstream Christians, eager to separate themselves from the Gnostics, thus avoided reference to Sophia.

Sophia and Feminist Spirituality

Following in the line of feminist theorists like Hélène Cixous and Luce Irigaray, the author's of Wisdom's Feast argue that in order to develop feminist spirituality we need to deconstruct traditional hierarchical binaries (i.e. sacred/profane, good/bad, male/female) and create a unity that celebrates the differentiation of its parts. Sophia, they insist, embodies this unity.

The orthodox or mainline church fight against this idea with such verses as Galatians 3:28, although that verse could also be seen as indicating the need for the balance they oppose.

New International Version

There is neither Jew nor Gentile, neither slave nor free, nor is there male and female, for you are all one in Christ Jesus.

It was the drive to keep things connected that was at the heart of the wisdom tradition. In the face of threats to Israel's national consciousness and to its provincial view of the world, the wisdom tradition sought to create a new more connected frame of reference. While groups within the priestly tradition in Israel and Judaism sought to separate and re-isolate the Hebrew faith, the wisdom tradition was trying to integrate the Hebrew perspective into the larger picture. (Cady et. al. 54)

Sophia was not only a force for unity within Judaism. She also established continuity between Judaism and Christianity. And her fusion with Christ offers contemporary Christians a way to understand their Savior as a union of male and female. As Mollenkott explains, "the combination of Wisdom/Christ leads to a healthy blend of male and female imagery that empowers everyone and works beautifully to symbolize the One God who is neither male nor female yet both male and female" (Mollenkott 104).

Similarly Johnson writes that through the filter of the Sophia metaphor, "new ways of appreciating Christ can be formed, less associated with patriarchal control and more in tune with women's daily life and collective wisdom, so often discounted as a source of insight" (Johnson 106). In light of this feminist revival of the Sophia figure, some Christian women have begun to speak of the "Sophia-God of Jesus" and of "Jesus Sophia."

Mollenkott also suggests that Sophia can replace the Virgin Mary as a positive role model for Catholic women. Mary, she insists, is an impossible model to follow, for no woman can be both virgin and mother. In addition, she argues that the strong, independent women of today cannot identify with Mary, for the Virgin Mother is a passive figure submissive to a masculine God. Sophia, however, may be a much more viable role model: "Dame Wisdom is an especially important symbol for contemporary women because she gets us beyond the concept that femaleness finds its primary fulfillment in motherhood. Wisdom is busy in the public sphere; she is no shrinking violet, no vessel waiting to be given her significance by someone else" (Mollenkott 102). Sophia supports a two-way flow of energy--both give and take--and thus she is an especially important figure for women who need to learn to restrain themselves from giving excessively.

However, like the Virgin Mary, Sophia too was shaped by a highly patriarchal society. In fact, some biblical portrayals of Dame Wisdom are clearly sexist. Some depictions of Sophia seem to reveal concerns that her growing power threatens patriarchal society. Proverbs 7 thus picks up on the traditional "bad girl" stereotype, describing Sophia as an evil harlot who threatens the patriarchally dominated institution of marriage.

Ultimately, the authors of Wisdom's Feast have to admit that much of the treatment of Sophia in the Bible and in the Christian tradition reinforces patriarchal values, making Sophia a potentially dangerous symbol of the divine. Too often she has played a mediating role, pointing toward God rather than to herself, and thus upholding male power. Because Sophia did not develop coequal status with Yahweh, because her voice is not identified in the Christian scriptures, it has been easy to keep her secondary and derivative. (Cady et. al. 13)

In more modern Gnostic groups, Sophia is talked about in relation to Eve, Mary, and Mary Magdalene. She is compared to Eve because both women experienced a "fall from grace" which resulted in the creation of the material world into the form it is today. In the myth she gives birth to a defective creature who she casts away, but who still retains power due to her holiness. In the end, most sources agree that Sophia can be developed into a positive figure for feminist spirituality.

Conclusion:

In more ways than one the Sophia figure suggests that the gender stratification of Judaism and Christianity is centered in the body. Most revealing is the name of this extremely powerful female figure of Judaism and Christianity. Her name "Wisdom" seems to lend her the power to transcend the "impurities" of her female body. Sophia's role in the Gnostic community also suggests that her power was rooted in her wisdom. Here, more divine than flesh and blood, she was capable of transcending any impurities that might have been associated with her female body. Although she was sometimes described as a mother of mankind and a lover of God, these were only metaphorical depictions of Sophia. Clearly her wisdom was manifested for mankind in the physical world.

The Sophia of Jesus and Eugnostos the Blessed

The similarity continues with the way both texts describe the Supreme Being as "indescribable ." Jesus says the word in response, however, to a question from Matthew. And so the two texts move along, with the Eugnostos the Blessed revealing how the universe emerged out of the "indescribable " Father. A series of Aeons (male and female) emanated from him. They, in turn, along with their assorted attendants, fill various heavenly realms. Eventually humans emerge. Their realm is called the realm of Immortal Man. In the Sophia of Jesus Christ, much of the same information unfolds in Jesus' answers to his disciples' questions.

The Father of the Universe, according to Eugnostos the Blessed, is more correctly referred to **not** as Father but as Forefather. The text discusses how that which comes from the imperishable will never perish but that which emerges from the perishable will die. These sections of the two texts are almost identical. Both texts conclude with the revelation that the Son of Man and his consort Sophia together show forth a light that is both great and androgynous — this light is the Savior. His masculine name is Savior, Father of All Things; his feminine name is Sophia, All Begetress (or Mother).

The Syrian and Egyptian schools of Gnosticism often featured in their doctrines an unknowable Supreme Being who emanated lesser beings called Aeons in pairs (male and female). These Aeons came forth in sequential order with the lowest of them being the Christ and Sophia pair. All together, they were seen as symbolizing the abstract nature of the Divine.

Joseph Lumpkin

Introduction of the Sophia of Jesus

The Sophia of Jesus Christ is dependent on and derived from the text called *Eugnostos the Blessed*, both of which were unearthed at Nag Hammadi. In the caves the archeologists found two copies for each book, but the copies differed somewhat.

The Sophia of Jesus Christ took the information and theology within *Eugnostos* and converted it into a dialogue with Jesus, placing the teachings of Eugnostos in the teaching of Jesus, spoken by him to his followers.

Scholars have referred to Eugnostos the Blessed and the Sophia of Jesus Christ as a revelation discourse in which the risen Christ answers his disciples' questions. Eugnostos the Blessed may have been composed during Jesus' lifetime or shortly thereafter and the Sophia of Jesus Christ seems to be near the end of the first century.

Eugnostos the Blessed opens as a letter with a formal greeting and goes on to proclaim that even the wisest philosophers have not understood the truth about the "ordering" of the world and that they have spoken three opinions, not agreeing. The Sophia of Jesus Christ opens after Jesus has risen and his twelve disciples and some women go up on a mountain called Divination and Joy. There the Savior appears and tells them that their speculation about the world

The Sophia of Jesus and Eugnostos the Blessed

order has not reached the truth, nor has it been reached by the three ways the philosophers have put forth.

Douglas M. Parrott, in his translation for the book, *The Nag Hammadi Library in English,* edited by Robinson writes: "The notion of three divine men in the heavenly hierarchy appears to be based on Genesis 1-3 (Immortal Man = God; Son of Man = Adam [81,12]; Son of Son of Man, Savior = Seth). Because of the presence of Seth, although unnamed in the tractate, *Eugnostos* must be thought of as Sethian, in some sense. However, since it is not classically Gnostic and lacks other elements of developed Sethian thought, it can only be characterized as proto-Sethian. Egyptian religious thought also appears to have influenced its picture of the supercelestial realm. The probable place of origin for *Eugnostos,* then, is Egypt. A very early date is suggested by the fact that Stoics, Epicureans and astrologers are called "all the philosophers." That characterization would have been appropriate in the first century B.C.E., but not later.

Eugnostos and *Soph. Jes. Chr.* may have influenced the Sethian-Ophites, as described by Irenaeus. Some have proposed an influence by *Eugnostos* on Valentinianism. Because of the dating of *Eugnostos,* it would not be surprising if *Soph. Jes. Chr.* had been composed soon after the advent of Christianity in Egypt - the latter half of the first century C.E. That possibility is supported by the tractate's relatively nonpolemical tone."

The translation of "The Sophia of Jesus Christ," also called "The Wisdom of Jesus Christ," is derived from two separately preserved copies of the text. The first copy is in Nag Hammadi Codex III (NHC III); a second copy of this text was preserved in the Berlin Gnostic Codex. A third fragment of the text in Greek was also found among the Oxyrhynchus papyrus documents. Thus we have three distinct copies of this scripture attested from three separate ancient sources, two in Coptic, one in Greek.

The mythologies preserved in the Nag Hammadi documents are dated to about the second century A.D. and are built on the assumptions and concepts of Plato and the philosophers who followed him. They elaborated on the creation of the universe in Plato's *Timaeus*.

The Sophia's main sources, *Eugnostos the Blessed*, is replete with Platonisms. The cosmology and theology of Plato, combined with Christian ideas gave us Christian Gnosticism and the degree of Platoisms within the Gnostic system gave rise to various Gnostic "denominations." Generally Gnosticism is considered a type of Christianity but there were Gnostics that were not Christians. These held to the belief that one had to receive knowledge or gnosis to see the true nature of the world and thus escape but they did not hold to the belief that Jesus or Jesus alone was sent to impart that gnosis. The revelation could come from a teacher or from the indescribable God directly. This seems to be the type of Gnosticism presented in

The Sophia of Jesus and Eugnostos the Blessed

Eugnostos the Blessed. One could see how this, by adding the exclusive conduit of Jesus, could become a Christian Gnostic text.

Both *Eugnostos* and *The Sophia* list the main emanations or beings that came to constitute the perfect, spiritual realm along with the Forefather. These beings include the "Self-Father" (the image of the Forefather as if viewed in a mirror), the "Immortal Man" who had the balance of male and female power. It is this entity who emerges in the beam of light as the Forefather views his/her image, the "Son of Man," who is the first-*begotten*, meaning the others were not begotten, and the "Savior," who is "revealed" by the Son of Man as a "great light," having both male and female energies. Each of these figures are endowed with both male and female energies and have their corresponding "female" portion, usually called "Sophia" or Wisdom.

The Sophia of Jesus Christ places the whole letter of instruction with Eugnostos the Blessed into the form of a dialogue between "the Saviour", Jesus the Christ, and his disciple *Eugnostos*, who at the time of the teaching from Jesus showed no signs of being "Christian."

Most Gnostic systems in and around Syria or Egypt taught that the universe began with an original, unknowable God, referred to as the Indescribable God, Parent God, Bythos, the Monad, the Unity or the One. God is looked at as a divine light and from light souls are formed. The One spontaneously emanated and created Aeons.

These are beings we would consider angels or demons. They were created in pairs and as the light shown, it traveled forth and as it diminished it begat or produced through its emanation progressively 'lesser' beings in sequence as it went forth. Each being was farther away from the source and was less in some way as the one before.

As the beings were created, so was their abode with the creator in the midst. The place, which we would view as heaven, is called the Pleroma, or fullness of God. Since God is in the Pleroma it is symbolic of being in or with the divine nature.

According to some Gnostic texts, Sophia, one of the first and most powerful Aeons, wished to know or unite with the indescribable God. Depending on the mythos, she either tried to emulate God and attempted to create on her own, without help or consent, or she attempted to breach the barrier between herself and the unknowable One. After failing, she was ejected from the Pleroma and was then in a fallen state.

Sophia's misplaced desires gave rise to matter and soul. The first-born and most powerful result of her disaster is the Demiurge whose name is Yaldabaoth, "Son of Chaos." Sophia saw the grotesqueness of her mistake and flung her creation away from her. The Demiurge, being alone, perceived himself to be his own creator and the ultimate power. He then began to create Aeons of his own.

The Sophia of Jesus and Eugnostos the Blessed

He and his Aeons created the physical universe in which we live, including man. Man was created imperfect from the imperfect god. The Demiurge did not have the power, or possess enough of the divine spark of life to fully complete the task. Man was produced in the form of a worm. Sophia looked on man and had pity, feeling responsible for him since it was her mistake that brought the pitiful creature to life. Sophia infused some of her divine spark or pneuma into man.

In another Gnostic text. The Pistis Sophia, Christ is sent from the Godhead in order to bring Sophia back into the fullness (Pleroma). Christ enables her to again see the light, bringing her knowledge of the spirit. Christ is then sent to earth in the form of the man Jesus to give men the Gnosis needed to rescue themselves from the physical world and return to the spiritual world. In Gnosticism, the Gospel story of Jesus itself is an allegory. It is considered the Outer Mystery or first mystery and is used as an introduction to Gnosis.

For the Gnostics, the drama of the redemption of the Sophia through Christ must be repeated in all of us. The word of God must call out to the wisdom in all of us and enable us to see the truth and find our way back to the one true God. The Sophia resides in all of us as the Divine Spark to be fanned to flame with the truth Christ delivers.

Jews in Alexandria, being heavily influenced by Greek philosophy, were occupied with the concept of the Divine Sophia, as the revelation of God's wisdom and feminine voice or force. They believed she was involved in the formation and running of the natural universe. She was responsible for communicating divine insight and knowledge to mankind. It was easy and natural for the fascination and reverence for Sophia to influence new Christians in the area, since they made up the majority of the new Jesus sect of Judaism.

In Proverbs 8, Sophia or Wisdom is described as God's Counselor and Work-mistress. The Revised Version has it as "Workmen" but the noun is feminine. She dwelt beside Him before the Creation of the world and was with Him.

Proverbs 8
Douay-Rheims 1899 American Edition (DRA)
8 Doth not wisdom cry aloud, and prudence put forth her voice?
2 Standing in the top of the highest places by the way, in the midst of the paths.
3 Beside the gates of the city, in the very doors she speaketh, saying:
4 O ye men, to you I call, and my voice is to the sons of men.
5 O little ones, understand subtilty, and ye unwise, take notice.
6 Hear, for I will speak of great things: and my lips shall be opened to preach right things.
7 My mouth shall meditate truth, and my lips shall hate wickedness.
8 All my words are just, there is nothing wicked nor perverse in them.
9 They are right to them that understand, and just to them that find knowledge.

The Sophia of Jesus and Eugnostos the Blessed

10 Receive my instruction, and not money: choose knowledge rather than gold.

11 For wisdom is better than all the most precious things: and whatsoever may be desired cannot be compared to it.

12 I wisdom dwell in counsel, and am present in learned thoughts.

13 The fear of the Lord hateth evil: I hate arrogance, and pride, and every wicked way, and a mouth with a double tongue.

14 Counsel and equity is mine, prudence is mine, strength is mine.

15 By me kings reign, and lawgivers decree just things,

16 By me princes rule, and the mighty decree justice.

17 I love them that love me: and they that in the morning early watch for me, shall find me.

18 With me are riches and glory, glorious riches and justice.

19 For my fruit is better than gold and the precious stone, and my blossoms than choice silver.

20 I walk in the way of justice, in the midst of the paths of judgment,

21 That I may enrich them that love me, and may fill their treasures.

22 The Lord possessed me in the beginning of his ways, before he made any thing from the beginning.

23 I was set up from eternity, and of old before the earth was made.

24 The depths were not as yet, and I was already conceived. neither had the fountains of waters as yet sprung out:

25 The mountains with their huge bulk had not as yet been established: before the hills I was brought forth:

26 He had not yet made the earth, nor the rivers, nor the poles of the world.

27 When he prepared the heavens, I was present: when with a certain law and compass he enclosed the depths:

28 When he established the sky above, and poised the fountains of waters:
29 When he compassed the sea with its bounds, and set a law to the waters that they should not pass their limits: when be balanced the foundations of the earth;
30 I was with him forming all things: and was delighted every day, playing before him at all times;
31 Playing in the world: and my delights were to be with the children of men.

Based on the above verse, and other sources, Gnostics gave a special place to Sophia, and her relation to the physical world.

In the time of the Gnostics only seven planets were known. They were thought of as seven circles rising one above another, and dominated by the seven Archons. These constituted the (Gnostic) Hebdomad. The Hebdomad is the seven "world-creating" archons in most Gnostic systems. Above the highest of them, and over-vaulting it, was the Ogdoad, the sphere of immutability, which was next to the spiritual.

Sophia's position is further defined in Proverbs 9.

Proverbs 9
Douay-Rheims 1899 American Edition (DRA)

9 Wisdom hath built herself a house, she hath hewn her out seven pillars.
2 She hath slain her victims, mingled her wine, and set forth her table.

3 She hath sent her maids to invite to the tower, and to the walls of the city:
4 Whosoever is a little one, let him come to me. And to the unwise she said:
5 Come, eat my bread, and drink the wine which I have mingled for you.
6 Forsake childishness, and live, and walk by the ways of prudence.
7 He that teacheth a scorner, doth an injury to himself: and he that rebuketh a wicked man, getteth himself a blot.
8 Rebuke not a scorner lest he hate thee. Rebuke a wise man, and he will love thee.
9 Give an occasion to a wise man, and wisdom shall be added to him. Teach a just man, and he shall make haste to receive it.
10 The fear of the Lord is the beginning of wisdom: and the knowledge of the holy is prudence.
11 For by me shall thy days be multiplied, and years of life shall be added to thee.
12 If thou be wise, thou shalt be so to thyself: and if a scorner, thou alone shalt bear the evil.
13 A foolish woman and clamorous, and full of allurements, and knowing nothing at all,
14 Sat at the door of her house, upon a seat, in a high place of the city,
15 To call them that pass by the way, and go on their journey:
16 He that is a little one, let him turn to me. And to the fool she said:
17 Stolen waters are sweeter, and hid den bread is more pleasant.
18 And he did not know that giants are there, and that her guests are in the depths of hell.

Based on the above verse, Gnostic believed Sophia had her house above the created universe, in the place of the midst, between the upper and lower world. She sits at "the gates of the mighty," at the realms of the seven Archons, and at the "entrances" to the upper realm of light her praise is sung. Sophia is therefore the highest ruler over the visible universe, and at the same time the mediatrix between the upper and the lower realms. She is "the mother of the living," from which all souls draw their beginning and creation. By her the light is brought down from the pleroma in order to light the darkness of the physical world.

Sophia was with God and lost her first estate. She lost her memory of God and had to be restored to her rightful place by Jesus, who came to "re-teach" her the things she once knew. The fate of Sophia is the prototype of what is repeated in the history of all individual souls, which, being of a heavenly origin, have fallen from the upper world of light, which was their original home. Souls should have remembered their origins because they have the divine spark from God in them, which came through Sophia, but they came under the influence of evil powers, from whom they must endure suffering until they return to the upper world once more.

Sophia needed the redemption through Christ, by whom she is delivered from her ignorance and was then brought back to her original home in the Upper Pleroma. The souls of all her children must follow her example and be returned to heaven. There, in the heavenly bridal chamber, they will all celebrate the marriage feast of eternity.

Being armed with a surface knowledge of Gnosticism we can proceed to the texts, which we are now equipped to better understand.

The Sophia of Jesus Christ
Also Called
The Wisdom of Jesus Christ

Following the resurrection of Jesus, the twelve, along with seven women, continued to be his disciples, and went to Galilee to the mountain called "Seeking Knowledge and Joy".

When they gathered together they were baffled and had questions concerning the nature and structure of the universe, the intended plan of redemption, God's protection and intention, and the power of the spiritual rulers. The disciples had questions about the mysteries the Savior had taught them in secret.

It was at this point the Savior appeared. He did not appear in his previous form, but in the form of an invisible spirit. And his likeness was like an immense angel of light. But what he looked like I must not describe. No earthly flesh could endure it, but only pure and perfect flesh, the nature of which he taught us about on the Mount of Olives, in Galilee.

And he said: "Peace be to you, My peace I give you!" They were amazed and frightened but the Savior laughed and said to them:

The Sophia of Jesus and Eugnostos the Blessed

"What are you thinking about? What are the questions perplexing you?"

Philip said: "We do not understand the underlying reality of the universe, the plan of redemption, or the meaning of the mysteries."

The Savior replied to them: "I want you to understand that every person born on earth from the beginning of the world until now were mortal (dust / animal). They sought God and had questions about who he is and about his nature, but none found him.

The wisest among these types of men have speculated about the way the world works and about its movement. But their speculations have not brought them to the truth. All this speculation has culminated into three philosophies and their philosophers do not agree.

Some say the world directs itself. Others say that it is the hand of God that directs it. Others say that it is fate. But none of these three views are close to being the truth. They are mere speculation and are in error.

(Note: Of the three philosophies, some think the world runs like a clock, once wound up or created, it runs itself without guidance from man or god. Some believe god controls each situation and event. Some believe it is not controlled at all, but life is simply a series of random events.)

I know "He who is Infinite Light" and I have come from him to teach you about the nature of life and to teach you the truth.

Mortal life which comes from mortal life is unclean. Fate and randomness have no wisdom and do not discern between people. But you have been chosen to know the truth and if you are worthy of this knowledge you will receive it and understand it. Whoever has not been conceived and born from the act of carnal sex (literally: whoever has not been sown by the act of rubbing flesh together in uncleanness) but instead has been begotten by the First Born who was sent, he will be an immortal being in the midst of mortal men."

Matthew said to him: "Lord, no one can find the truth except through you. So, we ask you to teach us the truth (so we can know your source)."

The Savior said: "He Who Is indescribable cannot be known by anything or anyone made. Nothing created can know him. No idea can fathom him. From the beginning of the world until now, he has not been revealed or understood by anyone except himself alone and those to whom he wishes to reveal himself, and that revelation comes through "He Who is From the Source of Light."

From this point forward, it is I who am the Great Savior, and I will teach you about the source of light. He is immortal and eternal. He is eternal because he was not born, for everyone was was born or shall be born will perish. He was not conceived and has no beginning. All who have a beginning will have an end.

He has no name. All creatures (things created or born) have a name and are the creation of some other person or creature. He comes from no one and no one rules over him.

He cannot be named. You cannot know his nature. He has no body, for whoever has human form is the creation of another person."

"He resembles no one but himself. He is unlike anything or anyone you have ever seen or perceived. His visage exceeds anything in the universe.

He is infinite and is the only thing in the universe that can see all aspects of himself. No mind can grasp him. He is immortal and looks like nothing anyone has ever seen. He is unchanging good, perfect and eternal. He is holy. Even though he cannot be known, he knows himself and he is omniscient. He cannot be quantified or measured. He is blessed, sacred, timeless, flawless, eternal and he is called 'Father of the Universe'".

Philip said: "Lord, how did god reveal himself to the perfect ones?" The perfect Savior answered: "Before all that is seen became visible, the power and authority were his. He contained the unity and entirety of all things, and there was nothing outside of him. He is mind and thought, consideration, memory, rationality and power.

All of these parts had equal authority and value since they were all from the source of his total mind. Before the beginning the eternal Father knew the entire race of the perfect ones, from first one to last one."

(Note: The reader must keep in mind that even though we are socially comfortable in referring to god as "he" the Gnostics gave god both male and female attributes equally. These attributes or energies are expressed in the following dialog.)

Thomas asked him: "Master and Savior, why were they created, and why were they revealed?"
The perfect Savior responded: "I came to you from infinity so that I can explain all things to you. The Existent Spirit was the father, who had the power to beget (like a father) and also had the nature to give form to creation (like a mother). He did this because he wished to reveal the vast wealth that was hidden within him. Because of his mercy and love, he wished to bring forth fruit by himself, so he did not have to experience goodness alone.

He wished other perpetual spirits to bring forth flesh and fruit in a glorious and upright way, in order to show his eternal and infinite grace so that the treasures of Self-Created God, the father of every eternal thing, might be revealed by those that came into existence afterward. But they had not yet been made visible and great differences existed among the eternal beings."

The Sophia of Jesus and Eugnostos the Blessed

He cried out, announcing: "Whoever has ears to hear about the things of infinity, let him hear! I speak to you who are awake."

He continued and said: "Everything that came from that which will perish will itself perish. Like begets like. But whatever came from that which will not perish will not perish but it will be eternal. Many men went missed their aim because they did not know the difference before they died."

Mary asked him: "Lord, how can we really know what you have taught us?"
The perfect Savior said: "You originated from the place of invisible things and came into the realm of visibility. Those who belong to Unbegotten Father, The emanation of pure thought, will understand through his revelation how faith in the invisible realm is found in those that are visible. Whoever has ears to hear, let him hear!

(Note: Gnostics believe that the creator of the visible realm is not the Lord of the universe. The creator of the visible realm was the Demiurge. Thus if the Demiurge was the "father" of the physical realm the Lord of the Universe would be called the forefather, since the forefather created Sophia and Sophia created the Demiurge. This means both Sophia and the Demiurge have a beginning and creator, but the Lord of the Universe is without a beginning.)

And he continued: "The Lord of the Universe should not be called 'Father', but he should be called 'Forefather', because he is the beginning of those that will appear. The Lord has no beginning, so he is called the Forefather. "

(Note: The following paragraphs are difficult to understand if one is not a Gnostic of the first century. They seem convoluted but represent an attempt to explain how the "Prime Causality" or the "Forefather" became both Forefather and Son of God by producing his own image.)

He continued, saying: "Seeing himself within himself as in a mirror, he resembled no one but himself, and his appearance was as the Holy Father for he is the father of himself. He is watcher who is viewing the watched one, and he was the First in Existence and the Father who was never begotten. He is equal to himself in age, for he is the Light facing the same Light, but he is not equal to him in power."

Then an entire multitude begot themselves and they were equal in age, power, and glory, and they were innumerable, and the race was called 'The Generation Ruled By No Kingdom.'

It was from one of these that mankind appeared. Those in that multitude over which there is no kingdom are called 'Sons of Unbegotten Father, God, Savior, and Son of God.'

You have his likeness. He is the unknowable, and full of eternal ever-lasting glory and indescribable joy. All are at rest in him,

The Sophia of Jesus and Eugnostos the Blessed

rejoicing in indescribable joy forever in his eternal glory and they celebrate greatly such as was never heard or known among any of the aeons or their worlds until now."

Matthew said to him: "Master and Savior, how was Man manifested?"

The perfect Savior responded: "I taught you that he who came into being existed before the universe. He is infinite. He made and grew from himself because he is full of light, bright and indescribable. From the beginning he decided to have his image become a great power. When he decided this, immediately The Source of Light appeared as an Immortal Man, having both male and female attributes and energies. It is through that Immortal Androgynous Man people might attain their salvation and awaken from their forgetfulness. The one who was sent to teach you and explain this to you is now with you until the end of the poverty, which the robbers have brought upon you.

And his consort is the Great Sophia, who was created from the beginning in him and for him to be united with him. The immortal, self-created divine king and father revealed this. And he created a great aeon, whose name is 'Ogdoad', for his own majesty."

(Note: Valentinius was a prominent second century Gnostic leader. He used the term Ogdoad to describe eight emanations - grouped in pairs of male/female, active/passive principles - by which Creation was effected. Initially there was the masculine principle of Bythos (the Abyss or Depth which was boundless and unqualified) from which came the feminine Silence, Grace or Thought. The uniting of these two produced Mind (masculine) and Truth (feminine). These four principles are the root of everything. The powers brought forth further powers called Aeons, which were produced in masculine/feminine pairs. The union of Mind and Truth brought forth Word (logos), which was masculine, and Life, which was feminine. Together they created Man (masculine) and the Church (feminine). This group of eight principles formed the Ogdoad, which in turn produced further Aeons. The thirtieth of these was Sophia. Her desire for wisdom drove her attempt to know god in ways she was not capable of. The error of Sophia in not comprehending her limits. Her error that caused the Fall that made our Universe, according to Valentinian myth. Later, some Gnostic would apply the term to Jesus. According to the Gnostics, most people are asleep and do not realize that there exists a higher spiritual reality. They sleepwalk, seeing only the lower manifestations and assume there is nothing more. Through gnosis brought about by Jesus it is possible for the higher Mind (logos) to discern the true nature of reality. Jesus would be the Ogdoad, and the expression of this higher knowledge.)

"He was given full authority to rule over the creation of poverty. He created gods and angels, archangels, and innumerable myriads of creatures, and they accompanied him. From that Light and the tri-male Spirit, which is that of Sophia, his consort they were made. But God was the source of divinity and the kingdom, and therefore he was called 'God of gods' and 'King of kings'.

This "First Man" has God's unique mind. He is like God within and in his thought. This is because he is the thought, consideration, reflection, rationality, and power of God. All the attributes that exist are perfect and immortal. As God is eternal, so is the First man and they are equal in mind and immortality but not in power. In power (authority) they are different, like the difference between father and son. As I said earlier, among the things that were created, the monad is first."

(Note: When the texts indicates the "First Son" is not equal to God in power we must consider this, not as power of creation or destruction, but more in the area of authority. A son may be as strong as the father but the father will have more authority than the son. Think about the difference in degree of authority between a king and a prince.)

"And at the conclusion everything was manifested from his power. And from that which was created everything was fashioned, from what was fashioned everything was formed, and from everything that was formed everything was named. And this how there arose differences among the unbegotten ones from beginning to end."

Then Bartholomew said to him: " In the Gospel 'Man' and 'Son of Man' are mentioned? To which of them is this Son related?"

The Holy One said to him: "I taught you The First Man is called 'The One Who Begets`, and `Self-perfected Mind'. He and the Great Sophia, his consort, reflected together and manifested his first-begotten son who contains both male and female energies. His male name is 'First Father, and Son of God', his female name is 'First Woman who Begat, Sophia, Mother of the Universe'. Some call her 'Love'. Now First-begotten is called 'Christ'. Since he has authority from his father, he created an innumerable multitude of angels who accompany the Spirit and Light."

His disciples said to him: "Lord, teach us about the one called 'Man', that we also may completely know his glory."

The perfect Savior said: "Whoever has ears to hear, let him hear. First Father is called 'Adam, Eye of Light.' He is called this because he came from shining Light. The Light's holy angels have no shadow and are beyond description, and they rejoice with joy forever as they reflect what they received from their Father.

The entire Kingdom of "Son of Man", who is called 'Son of God,' is indescribably joyous and constant jubilation. It is without shadow and in it there is rejoicing forever over His eternal glory. The likes of such a celebration has never been heard until now, nor have the aeons that came afterward or any of their worlds experienced anything like it. I came to you from self-created one who is the first and infinite light, that I might reveal everything to you."

Once again, his disciples questioned him, saying: "Explain to us how they came down from the invisible, immortal world to the mortal world."

The perfect Savior said: "Son of Man consented with Sophia, his consort, and manifested a great light, having both male and female components. His male name is called 'Savior, Father of All Things'. His female name is called 'Mother of All, Sophia (wisdom)'. Some call her 'Faith'.

"All who come into the world are like a single drop from the Light. They are sent to the world of the Almighty Light in order to be guarded by the Light. The Almighty Light bound the drops with forgetfulness through the power he retained from Sophia's will during her creation of him. He did this so that the matter might be spread through the whole world in poverty, and "Almighty" may continue in his arrogance and blindness and ignorance, which befit his real name (Yaldaboth).

But I came from the realms above by the will of the great Light. I escaped from his bond. I have brought the work of the robbers to a halt. I have awakened those drops that were sent from Sophia, so that they might bear much fruit through me.
 They can now be perfected and never again go back to their defective state.

Through me, the Great Savior, the glory of the true god will be revealed, so that Sophia might regain her state from the defective state she initiated, and her sons might not again become defective but might attain honor and glory and be able to go to their Father, and know the words of the masculine Light.

And you were sent by the Son, and the Son was sent so that you might receive Light, and remove yourselves from the induced state of forgetfulness brought about by the rulers here. And I am here so that the condition might not overtake you again or be manifested again because when you have sex that comes from the fire and fear that came from the flesh it produces distorted malicious intent, and this is the intent of the rulers."

Then Thomas said to him: "Lord, Savior, how many aeons are in the realms above the heavens (sky)?"
The perfect Savior said: "I am proud of all of you because you asked me about the great aeons. It shows me that your roots are in the infinite. When those whom I have discussed with you earlier were revealed, Self-created Father very soon created twelve aeons to accompany the twelve angels. All these are perfect and good, but the defect (imbalance) in the female appeared."

And Thomas said to him: "How many immortal aeons came from the infinite?"

The Sophia of Jesus and Eugnostos the Blessed

The perfect Savior said: "Whoever has ears to hear, let him hear. The first aeon is the Son of Man, who is called 'First Father' and he is called 'Savior' and he has appeared. The second aeon is Man, who is called 'Adam, Eye of Light'. The aeon covering him has no kingdom. He is the aeon of the Eternal Infinite God, the Self-created aeon and is over the aeons. He is the aeon of the immortals, whom I described earlier. He is the aeon above the Seventh, which appeared from Sophia, which is the first aeon.

"Now Immortal Man manifested aeons and powers and kingdoms, and gave authority to all who appear in him, that they might exercise their desires until the last things that are above chaos. For these come together with each other and manifest everything considered magnificent. They brought about the light of spirit in a multitude of glorious manifestations and they are without number. These were called forth in the beginning by the first aeon who was first called 'Unity and Rest'.

Each Aeon has its own name but together they were called 'Assembly' because from the great multitude appeared in one aeon and in one aeon a multitude revealed themselves. Now because the multitudes gather and come to a unity we call them 'Assembly of the Eighth. They appeared with both male and female energies and attributes and were named partly as male and partly as female. The male is called 'Assembly', while the female is called 'Life', that it might be shown that from a female came the life for all the aeons. And from the beginning they were so named.

From the agreement of his thought, the powers appeared quickly and they were called 'gods'. And the gods of the gods from their wisdom manifested gods. From their wisdom they manifested masters and the masters of the masters through the power of their thoughts manifested archangels. Then archangels from their words revealed angels and from angles the outward appearances of reality manifested, with structure and form and name for all the aeons and their worlds."

"And the immortals, whom I have just described, all have authority passed to them from 'Immortal Man', who is called 'Silence', because through thought without speech all her own majesty was perfected. The immortals had power for each to create a great kingdom in the Eighth, and also thrones and temples and firmaments for their own majesties. For these all came into being through the will of the Mother of the Universe."

Then the Holy Apostles said to him: "Lord and Savior, it is necessary that we know, so please tell us about those who are in the aeons."

The perfect Savior said: "I will tell you about anything you ask. They created hosts of angels, myriads without number, for their accompaniment and for their glory. They created virgin spirits, the indescribable and unalterable lights. And through the strength of their will they have no sickness nor weakness."

"In this fashion the aeons were created rapidly in the heavens and the firmaments and contained the glory of "Immortal Man" and "Sophia," his consort. Their creation was patterned after the heavens of chaos and their worlds. This was their template. All natures, from the manifestation of chaos on are all in the Light that shines without shadow, and it contains joy that cannot be described, and unspeakable jubilation. They delight themselves forever because they have unchanging glory, all power, and rest without end. Even among the aeons this cannot be described. I have revealed this to you, I teach you this so you might shine in Light more than these."

Mary said to him: "Holy master, where did your disciples come from, and where are they going, and what is their purpose here?" The Perfect Savior said to them: "I taught you that Sophia, the Mother of the Universe and the consort, desired to bring these into existence by herself and without her male consort. She wanted to use the will of the Father of the Universe, (a part of which she contained) that his unfathomable goodness might be revealed. But he created that barrier between the immortals and those that came afterward, so that the consequence might follow.

Every aeon and chaos would show the defect of the female power alone, and the result would be that she would struggle with the error. And this error became the barrier of (for) spirit.

As I have taught you, it is from aeons above the emanations of Light that a drop from Light and Spirit came down to the lower regions of "Almighty" into chaos, that their fashioned forms might appear from that drop. The result is a judgment on him who is called "Arch-Father," and whose name is Yaldabaoth.

That drop manifested a fashioned form through the breath, as a living soul. But it was withered, misshapen and slept, as in a coma, and was ignorant of the soul. When it was heated from the breath of the Great Light of the Male it began to be able to think. Only then were names given by all who are in the world of chaos. All things in that realm of the soul came through that Immortal One when he breathed into him.

But when this came about by the will of "Mother Sophia", "Immortal Man" pieced together the garments by way of his breath, for a judgment on the robbers. But since he was like a soul himself, he was not able to take that power for himself until the number of the aeons of chaos was completed and the time determined by the great angel was fulfilled.

I have taught you about "Immortal Man" and in doing so I have freed you from the bonds of the robbers. I have done this for him. I have broken the gates of the cruel ones as they looked on. I have humiliated them and revealed their malicious intent. I have shamed them and forced them to face their ignorance.

I came here to do these things so that they have the opportunity to join with that Spirit and Breath and that they may be brought into unity and the two may become one, just as from the first. In this state of unity you will be fruitful and you will ascend to "Him Who Is from the Beginning", in unspeakable joy and glory and honor and grace of the Father of the Universe.

Whoever knows the Father in pure gnosis will ascend to the Father and rest in unborn Father. But whoever does not know him or has faulty error in their knowledge will go to the dwell in a defective state with those rejected from the Eighth. Now whoever knows "Immortal Spirit of Light in silence", through their thoughts and in their welcoming of the truth will show me proof they know of the Invisible One, and he will become a light in the Spirit of Silence. Whoever knows Son of Man in gnosis and love will bring me a sign of "Son of Man," and he will go to the dwelling-places with those in the Eighth.

Then he said: Behold, I have revealed to you the name of the "Perfect One" and the entire will of the Mother of the Holy Angels. I have shown you how the masculine multitude was completed. You have been told how the aeons appeared in the infinity and came to be in the unfathomable wealth of the Great Invisible Spirit and how they all took from his goodness, which was the treasure house of rest, which has no kingdom over it.

I came from First Who Was Sent, that I might reveal to you "Him Who Is from the Beginning." In their arrogance, "Arch-Father" and his angels thought they were gods. And I came to remove them from their blindness, that I might tell everyone about the God who is above the universe. I will stomp upon their graves, humiliate them, expose their malicious intent, and break their yoke. I will awaken my own. I have given you authority over all things as Sons of Light, that you might tread upon their power with your feet."

After the blessed Savior said these things he disappeared from them. Then all the disciples were greatly overjoyed in their spirit from that day on. And his disciples began to preach the Gospel of God, the eternal, immortal Spirit. Amen.

Introduction of Eugnostos The Blessed

In the Nag Hammadi library, two separate versions of Eugnostos The Blessed were found. Codex III and Codex V contained the tractate Eugnostos the Blessed and the two versions show some differences.

Codex III contains Eugnostos in its third document, occupying pages 70 -90. The first two lines of the text read, 'Eugnostos the blessed, to those who are his,' and the title at the end of the tractate is given as 'Eugnostos the Blessed.' For that reason the tractate is generally referred to as Eugnostos the Blessed. The opening of the version of the text in Codex V pages1-17 cannot be reconstructed in the same way, and the title at the conclusion of the document is merely 'Eugnostos.

The two versions are quite different from one another, and probably represent independent Coptic translations of a Greek original. The version in Codex III is usually taken to be an earlier version than the one in Codex V. In *The Nag Hammadi Library in English* the version in Codex III is the one chosen for translation, with missing or damaged portions supplemented by the version in Codex V.

Eugnostos is an interesting name. In Greek, *eugnostos* is an adjective composed of *eu*, 'good' or 'well,' and *gnostos*, 'known,' and so

Eugnostos means 'well known,' but could also mean 'easy to understand.' One should not interpret it as "easy to understand" without acknowledging the irony in the name, since the Gnostic concepts contained within the work are difficult to follow for the modern reader, unfamiliar with the subtleties of ancient Gnosticism.

The opposite of this term is *agnostos*, 'unknown,' a term commonly used in philosophy to indicate the supreme God. This adjective also has an active meaning, 'the one who can know,' 'the one capable of knowing' and is a play on the word and a synonym of the term *gnostes, meaning* 'the one who knows,' *Acts*26:3). Those who are Gnostic are gnostes. The link between *gnostos* and *gnostes* makes the name Eugnostos highly symbolic.

The name Eugnostos also appears in another Nag Hammadi document titled, *Holy Book of the Great Invisible Spirit*. In the final portion of this text the author introduces himself with his two names: Eugnostos, his spiritual name, and Gongessos, the name he would go by in his everyday life.

Eugnostos the Blessed is a philosophical treatise, if one could call Gnosticism a philosophy, rather than a theological treatise. It is presented in a letter written by Eugnostos to the readers as an explanation of the creation of gods in their realms and man.

The letter includes greetings to the recipients, and a formal conclusion.

The Sophia of Jesus and Eugnostos the Blessed

Eugnostos follows a clear train of thought in its attempt to explain its doctrine. It employs techniques of explanation and argument found in the philosophical schools of the time.

The letter contains a variety of material and doctrine, which may indicate the letter was changed or expanded in stages through time.

The author of *Eugnostos* opens with a criticism of philosophical theories (an allusion to Stoics, Epicureans, and Babylonian scholars) and proceeds to focus on truth as a divine revelation, not a human construction.

The author describes the divine realm inhabited by five beings, each having his own aeon and heavenly followers, angels, and deities. The exact names will vary depending on the way they are translated. These five beings are the (1) unborn, unbegotten or unconceived Father, (2) the Human Father by himself, (3) the Immortal Human or Immortal Man, (4) the Son of Humanity or the Son of Man, and (5) the Savior.

According to the author, *Eugnostos,* these beings were not produced through emanations, as is described in other Gnostic texts, but rather, they came into being as a continuous chain. The highest God, the unborn or unbegotten Father, is described by means of both negative theology with words and terms as "he cannot be described, indescribable , without name, infinite, incomprehensible, cannot be known, unchanging, imperishable, immortal, untraceable, and so on. He also uses positive theology, with words and phrases such as, he surpasses everything, and he is blessed, perfect, and the like. This way of approaching the notion of God was common in Middle Platonic schools and is employed in other Nag Hammadi texts. The *Secret Book of John* and *Allogenes the Stranger* also use this technique.

Eugnostosis was heavily influenced by Greek philosophical speculation and technique, but he also focuses on mystical Jewish elements. There is a deep interest in angelology but no particular preoccupation with angelic names and their pronunciation, as is generally seen in other Jewish pseudepigrapha, letters of Jewish mysticism, or other Nag Hammadi treatises.

Michel Tardieu concludes that *Eugnostos* "is a text which represents, for the history of thought, the first (in a temporal sense) expository treatise of revelation where metaphysics serves angelology and where angelology changes constantly into metaphysics."

Scopello states, "The original Greek text of *Eugnostos the Blessed* was probably composed in Egypt as early as the end of the first century. From Egypt this tractate circulated in Syria, and it was known in the school of Bardaisan in the beginning of the third century." (*The Nag Hammadi Scriptures*, p. 274)

Eugnostos the Blessed was most likely used to construct The Sophia of Jesus and when we look at Eugnostos we are likely seeing a Gnostic document, generally lacking in Christian theology and components, which was altered and expanded by the author of the Sophia of Jesus to render a book directed to the Gnostic Christian community. Thus, in Eugnostos we are able to go back one generation and see how the theology was altered and expanded.

To the readers of today, the main idea espoused within most Gnostic texts regarding creation may seem absurd and very tedious, as a "unbegotten" or "unborn" god spontaneously creates a being or beings via an unexplained emanation, only to have that creation then create others, who in turn also create, and on literally ad nauseam. To our scientific and critical minds, this action is best understood if one examines radio or sound waves. As a frequency is radiated, or emanated, the frequency produces harmonics, which are an integer multiple of the fundamental frequency. In turn the harmonics produce more harmonics, each one becoming less powerful as it is produced from the one before. The forth harmonic is usually less powerful than the second, as each is in turn farther away from the "source" or fundamental frequency. Each harmonic has the property of being a periodic of the fundamental frequency. In the same way the source of light and life in the Gnostic belief system produced beings, which in turn produced beings, each having less power as the creations are progressively farther removed from the source. Even though this insight will not mitigate the redundant creation patterns in the text, it will bring about a clearer understanding of the aim and purpose of the Gnostic explanation of creation.

Joseph Lumpkin

Eugnostos the Blessed

Eugnostos, the Blessed, to those who are in his care. Rejoice in the fact that you know (you have gnosis). Greetings!

I have taught you that all men born from the beginning of the world until now are dust. While they have searched and questioned about God, and wanted to know who he is and what he is like, they have not found him.

The wisest among them have speculated about the truth regarding how the world was formed and how it runs but their speculation has not brought them to the truth.

Three separate philosophers have opinions and have speculated about this and none agree. Some of them say the world runs by itself. Others say God directs it. Others, that it is fate and it is random. But none of these are correct.

Again, of three voices that I have just mentioned, none is true. For whatever is born from itself is an empty life; it is self-made.

The thought of providence is foolish.

The Sophia of Jesus and Eugnostos the Blessed

(Since "providence can mean god or nature this could be a statement that the "god of this world is foolish" or "leaving things to a natural outcome yields foolishness.")

Fate does not discern between people.

Whoever is able to break free of these three voices and listen to another voice and thus confess the God of truth and know (agree with) everything about him, that person will be an immortal dwelling in the midst of mortal men.

"He-Who-Is" is beyond description. No important person knew him, no authority or those subject to them, nor any creature from the beginning of the world knew him. Only he alone knew himself.

For he is immortal and eternal, having no birth; for everyone who is born will perish, but he was never born. He is unbegotten, having no beginning; for everyone who has a beginning has an end. No one rules over him. He has no name; for whoever has a name is the creation of another. He is unnameable. He has no human form; for whoever has human form is the creation of another. He has his own semblance - not like anything we have perceived or seen, but he has a strange, unfamiliar semblance that surpasses all things and is beyond anything and everything ever seen. (He is beyond infinity, thus) he looks to every side and sees himself from himself. He is infinite; he is incomprehensible. He is ever eternal and is unlike anything. He is unchanging good. He is faultless. He is everlasting.

He is blessed. He is unknowable and only he knows himself. He is immeasurable. He is untraceable. He is perfect and flawless. He is eternally blessed. He is called 'Father of the Universe'.

Before anything was visible among those that are visible, the majesty and the authorities were in him and he embraces the wholeness and totality of everything, and nothing embraces him. He is all mind, thought and reflection, consideration, rationality and power.

All these elements are equal powers. They are the sources of the totalities. And their whole race from first to last was in the foreknowledge of the Unbegotten, but they had not yet come to visible manifestation.

Now a difference existed among the immortal aeons. We know that everything that comes from something or someone perishable (mortal) will perish, since it came from something that will perish. Whatever came from immortal will not perish but will become immortal, since it came from immortality. Many men went astray because they did not known this difference, and thus they died.

(Note: The above text is an explanation of the Gnostic idea of salvation. A person must "denounce this world and all connections to the mortal, perishable world and realize his/her connection and path to the immortal, eternal, universal Father, from where we all originated. By doing so we achieve his same immortality in spirit.)

The Sophia of Jesus and Eugnostos the Blessed

This is all that needs to be said, since it is impossible for anyone to dispute the nature of my words about the blessed, immortal, true God.

Now, if anyone desires to have faith in the words I have set down here, let him go from here to the end of what is visible an discover what is hidden and invisible, and "Thought" will instruct him in how faith in those things that are not visible was found in what is visible. This is a principle of knowledge.

The Lord of the Universe is incorrectly called 'Father' but he is the 'Forefather'. For the Father is the beginning and real source of what is visible. For the Lord is without beginning and is the Forefather. He sees himself within himself, like a mirror, having appeared in his likeness as Self-Father, that is, Self-Father, and as he who stands before himself, since he is the Unborn (Unbegotten) First Existent one who stands before himself. He is indeed of equal age with the one who is before him, but he is not equal to him in power.

(Note: Set up two mirrors so an image seen in the first is reflected into both infinitively. All images are equal, but only the source image has the power.)

Afterward he revealed many self-begotten ones standing before him, equal in age and power, being in glory and without number, and they are called 'The Generation of Kingdoms over Whom There

Is No Kingdom'. And the whole multitude of that place, over which there is no kingdom, is called 'Sons of Unborn (Unbegotten) Father.'

Now the Unknowable One is forever full of immortal and indescribable joy. They all rest in him, rejoicing eternally in indescribable, unchanging measureless joy voiced in ceaseless jubilation that was never heard or known among all the aeons and their worlds. But, we should stop here, for we could go no forever describing the wondrous principles of the Father.

The first who appeared before the universe in infinity is the Self-created, Self-made Father, and he is full of shining, indescribable light. In the beginning, he decided his likeness should become a great power. Immediately, the source of light appeared as the Immortal Man, who had both male and female energies. His male name is 'Begotten, Perfect Mind'. And his female name is 'Mother Sophia', the all-wise one. It is said that she resembles her brother and her consort. She is uncontested truth. Yet, here, in the world below her world, error exists but her truth fights against it.

Through the Immortal Man appeared the first divisions of his choice, which were divinity and kingdom. This was because the Father, who is called 'The Self-Fathered Man' (self-begotten man) revealed this.

The Sophia of Jesus and Eugnostos the Blessed

He created a great aeon for his own majesty. He gave him great authority, and he ruled over all creations. He created gods and archangels and angels, myriads without number to attend him.

Now through that Man originated divinity and kingdom. Therefore he was called 'God of gods', 'King of kings'.

The "First Man" is 'Faith' ('pistis' is the Greek word for faith) for those who will come after him. Within him is a unique mind and thought. He is thought, reflection, consideration, rationality, and power. All the attributes that exist are perfect and immortal.

Certainly, they are equally immortal, but they are not equal in power, just as there is a difference in authority between a father and son. The son is the thought of the father, which remains.

I taught you earlier that of all the things that were created the "Unity," (indivisible, totality and oneness) was first and the (division) duality followed it, and after that, the triad followed it and divisions continued up to the tenth divisions and beyond. Those from the tenths rule the hundredths; the hundredths rule the thousandths; the thousands rule the ten thousands. This is the pattern of the immortals.

This is the pattern that exists among the immortals. The indivisible and the "Thought" are those things that belong to "the Immortal Man." The things that precede from thought belong to the tenths, and the teachings belong to the hundreds. Counsel belongs to the thousands. Power belongs to the ten thousands.

In the beginning, the mind produced thought and the things that came from thinking. Teaching came from these things and counsels came from teachings, and power came from counsels. Power manifested all the attributes; all that was manifested appeared from his powers, and everything created had form which was manifested from the attributes of power.

And what was formed appeared from what was created. What was named appeared from what was formed. This is when differences arose among begotten things, which appeared from what was named from the first to the last, by power of all the aeons. Now "The Immortal Man" is full of every eternal and indescribable glory and all joy. His whole kingdom rejoices in everlasting joy like no one ever heard or known in any aeon or world that came after them.

Afterward another principle came from "The Immortal Man," who is called 'The Self-perfected Father.' When he and his consort, Great Sophia were in agreement he revealed that first-begotten man, who had both male and female energies, who is called, 'The First-begotten Son of God'.

His female aspect is 'The First Born,' called Sophia, Mother of the Universe, and some call her 'Love'. The First-begotten, was given

The Sophia of Jesus and Eugnostos the Blessed

authority from his father to create countless angels to accompany and assist him. The entire gathering of those angels is called 'The Assembly of the Holy Ones," and the Lights without shadow.' When they greet one another their embraces become like the angels themselves.

The First Father is called 'Adam of the Light.' The kingdom of "The Son of Man" is full of indescribable joy and perpetual jubilation, and they rejoice forever in great joy for their eternal glory, which no aeon has heard, nor has it been revealed to any aeons that has ever existed.

Then Son of Man was in agreement with Sophia, his consort, and manifested a great Light, which is both male and female. His masculine name is called 'Savior, Father of All things'. His feminine name is called 'Sophia, The Mother of All' and some call her "Faith" (or Pistis in Greek).

Then the Savior was in agreement with his consort, Pistis Sophia, and revealed six spiritual beings, who were the type of those preceding them, having both male and female energies. Their male names are these:
The first, 'Unborn' (unbegotten); the second, 'Self-created' (self-begotten)'; the third, 'Father'; the fourth, 'First Father'; the fifth, 'All-Father'; and the sixth, 'Arch-Father'.

Also the names of the females are these; the first, 'All-wise Sophia'; the second, 'Mother of All - Sophia'; the third, 'All Wise Mother' (Mother of all Wisdom); the fourth, 'First Mother Sophia'; the fifth, 'Love Sophia'; and the sixth, 'Pistis Sophia (Faith – Wisdom)'.

Those I have just mentioned were in agreement and thoughts appeared in the aeons that exist. From thoughts came reflections (remembering); from reflections came considerations; from considerations came reason, from reason came will, and from will came words.

Then the twelve powers, whom I have just discussed, were in agreement with each other, males and females were revealed. Because of this, there are seventy-two powers. Each one of the seventy-two revealed five spiritual powers, which are the three hundred and sixty powers. When these all came together there was will.

These aeon came into existence as the type of Immortal Man. Now, time is a reflection of the types and came from the First Father, his son. The year is a type of Savior. The twelve months is the type of the twelve powers. The three hundred and sixty days is the type of the three hundred and sixty powers who appeared from Savior. Their hours are the type of the angels who came from them and moments are the type of the powers, who are without number.

The Sophia of Jesus and Eugnostos the Blessed

When all of these appeared, All-Father, their father, soon created twelve aeons to accompany the twelve angels. And in each aeon there were six heavens, producing a total of seventy-two heavens, for the seventy-two powers who appeared from him. Each heaven contained five firmaments, totaling three hundred sixty firmaments from the three hundred sixty powers that appeared from them. When the firmaments were completed, they were called 'The Three Hundred Sixty Heavens', because these were the name of the heavens that were before them. And all these are perfect, flawless and good. But this was the way the defect of separate female energy appeared.

The first aeon is "The Immortal Man". The second aeon is the "Son of Man", who is also called '"The First Father". It is he who is called "Savior". The one encompassing these is the aeon over which there is no kingdom. He is the Eternal Infinite God, the aeon of the aeon, and all immortals who are in the aeon above the Eighth that appeared in chaos.

The Immortal Man revealed aeons, powers and kingdoms and gave authority to everyone who appeared from him, so that they could make whatever they desire until the days of chaos come.

And these were in agreement with each other and manifested a multitude of splendid things from spirit and light and it was glorious. These received names in the beginning, that is, the first, the middle, the complete (perfect), which were the first aeon and the second and the third.

The first was called Unity and the second is Rest, since each one has its own name, and the third aeon is called 'Assembly'. A great multitude appeared in the one and in him there was a multitude. Therefore, when the multitude gathers in unity they are called 'Assembly', from the Assembly that is above heaven. Therefore, the Assembly of the Eighth was manifested both male and female energies and was named partly as male and partly as female. The male was called 'Assembly', the female was called 'Life'. This was to show that the female produced life in all the aeons. Then from the beginning all the names were received.

He agreed with his thought and the powers appeared who were called 'gods'; and from careful thoughts the gods revealed the divine gods; and from their deep thought the gods manifested lords; and the lords of the lords were formed from their words; and the lords from their powers produced archangels; the archangels made angels; from them, the likenesses appeared, with structure and form for naming all the aeons and their worlds.

All the immortals have authority from the power of Immortal Man and Sophia, his consort, who was also called 'Silence', because by reflecting without speech she perfected her own majesty. Since the immortals had the authority, and each produced a number of great kingdoms in all the eternal heavens and their firmaments, thrones and temples, to demonstrate their own majesty.

Some are in buildings and chariots, which were indescribable in their glory so that no creature could attain them. And hosts of angels without number were made by these aeons in order to accompany them in glory and the angels were spirits of unimaginable light, perpetual in their virginity. They are pure will, having no sickness nor weakness, and they come into being instantaneously. In this way the aeons with their heavens and firmaments for the glory of Immortal Man and Sophia, his consort came into being.

The pattern of every aeon and their worlds and those that came afterward are herein contained in order to provide the types. And from the chaos of the world their likenesses were revealed in the heavens.

From the Immortal One, who is Unbegotten, to the revelation of chaos, everything is in the light that shines without shadow in indescribable joy and jubilation without words. They are eternally delighted because of their glory that does not change, and the complete rest, which cannot be described. No aeons that came to be nor any of their powers can conceive of the depth of glory or rest. But this much is enough, that you might accept these things until the one who does not need be taught appears among you. Then he will speak all these things to you with zeal and in purity of knowledge.

The Sophia of Jesus and Eugnostos the Blessed

www.ingramcontent.com/pod-product-compliance
Lightning Source LLC
Chambersburg PA
CBHW061946070426
42450CB00007BA/1064